IMAGES
of America

MOCKSVILLE

MOCKSVILLE TOWN PLAT. Thomas McNeely drew the Mocksville town plan in 1837. Business lots sold at public auction with proceeds funding construction of the courthouse and jail. Note that the plat shows Main Street as Henderson Street and Depot Street as Factory Street. McNeely arrived in Mocksville around 1820 and established himself as a merchant, farmer, and owner of a steam-powered cotton factory and a blacksmith shop. He served as magistrate of the first county court in 1837, first chairman of the board of commissioners in 1839, and postmaster from 1830 to 1847.

ON THE COVER: Mocksville's fourth war bond rally on February 12, 1944, attracted about 3,500 people and raised over $17,000 in war bonds.

IMAGES
of *America*

MOCKSVILLE

Debra Leigh Dotson and Jane Satchell McAllister

ARCADIA
PUBLISHING

Published by Arcadia Publishing
Charleston, South Carolina

Library of Congress Control Number: 2010928091

For all general information, please contact Arcadia Publishing:
Telephone 843-853-2070
Fax 843-853-0044
E-mail sales@arcadiapublishing.com
For customer service and orders:
Toll-Free 1-888-313-2665

Visit us on the Internet at www.arcadiapublishing.com

*The authors gratefully dedicate this book to county historian James Wall,
whose lifelong interest and guidance ensure that the stories continue*

CONTENTS

ACKNOWLEDGMENTS

The authors gratefully acknowledge the following people who shared their photographs: Dean Allen, Bert Bahnson, James Barringer, John Caudle, Clemmons Branch of the Forsyth County Public Library system, C. C. Craven, Davidson College Archives, Frances Collette Dunn, Bill Ferebee, Forsyth County Public Library Photograph Collection, John Fuller, Peter W. Hairston, Lester P. Martin Jr., Hugh S. Larew, Carol and Lisa LeGrand, Polly Lomax, Gwynn Meroney, Jack Pennington, Gene Plott, Marie Roth, Rowan Museum, *Salisbury Post*, Lash and Cyrette Sanford, Taylor Slye, Charles "Muggs" Smith, Estelle Smith, Gwyn and Ann Smith, Robin Snow, Robert Stafford, Ray Tutterow, James Wall, Betty Etchison West, Ron Williams, and Edith Shutt Zimmerman. Unless otherwise noted, all images appear courtesy of the Davie County Public Library. The authors regret being unable to use all photographs submitted due to limited space.

INTRODUCTION

Deciphering the history of a place requires sifting through official government documents such as deeds, tax and estate records, and court minutes. Publications from the time period offer significant insights into commerce, social and economic life, and prominent people. Old photographs offer additional, much more subjective, and evocative evidence of the way we lived and worked in years past. This book shares the photographic story of the development of the town of Mocksville and its people up to roughly the mid-1900s.

Named the county seat of the newly created Davie County in 1839, the town of Mocksville, originally known as Mocks Old Field, may have existed as early as the Revolutionary War. The Rowan Court in 1783 summoned local landowner Andrew Mock to defend against confiscation of his land for his Tory sympathies during the war. Mock purchased 250 acres from Casper Sain in 1785; at least part of this land fell within the town limits established for Mocksville. The year of 1810 saw the creation of the Mocks Old Field Post Office.

A March 3, 1837, deed records the sale and conveyance by Archibald G. Carter and wife Letitia, Thomas McNeely, and Wiley Lowery of 19.25 acres of land to the Davie County Court for a sum of $234.40. County commissioners reported three years later on the division of the land into 32 business lots, which sold at public auction for $11,582.50. Col. Henry Austin contracted to build the courthouse and jail for $11,312, freeing the new county from any imposition of taxes for the construction. The business section of town relocated from Salisbury Street to the downtown square. Early bylaws of the Town of Mocksville, as recorded in the minutes of the Commissioners Meetings of 1845, included prohibitions against stopping and feeding teams on the square, horse racing, and leaving livestock or vehicles on the street at night. A fine of $10 was assessed on "any manager of a circus or menagerie who performed within the corporate limits."

Official records and newspapers speak of various trades practiced in the town. As noted in the *Western Carolinian* of April 25, 1839, "Mocksville had six Dry Goods stores, one Confectionary, two excellent houses for public entertainment, one excellent Female Academy taught by Miss Emily Alden, one Tobacco factory, one steam sawmill, one cotton factory, two Cabinet warehouses, two Tanning yards, two shoe shops, two tailor shops, three blacksmith shops, and one hat shop." Often enough evidence can be gleaned to tell a rich story of such businesses. Other times, we crave more than just the briefest mention of an early business. The *Carolina Watchman* of April 17, 1846, stated, "Isaac A. Witherspoon of Mocksville, carriage builder, passed through Salisbury with six of his new vehicles. An experienced man in his line, he possesses the skill of combining the beautiful with the substantial in his jobs."

Mocksville, and Davie County as a whole, remained a rural, largely agriculturally based economy. Bright leaf tobacco replaced cotton as the leading cash crop in the mid-1800s, and farm acreage increased significantly. Family farms produced their own food, which included a variety of vegetables and meat, especially pork. Agriculture continues as an important component of the local economy today.

Records cannot tell us much of private residences; photographs best preserve such memories. Although many beautiful older homes remain in Mocksville, this book provides evidence of the passing parade of homes that did not survive.

Early European settlers erected school buildings upon their arrival in the mid- to late 1700s. Several well-regarded private academies operated in the area in the 1800s, including Sunnyside Seminary, whose pupils were taught by Mattie Eaton and Laura Clement. Sunnyside commencements under the Baptist arbor in North Mocksville attracted hundreds of spectators according to Mary J. Heitman, a Sunnyside pupil. Mocksville Academy still stands on Salisbury Street, one of the area schools at which Peter Stuart Ney, a schoolteacher with a mysterious past, taught. Few families could afford such subscription-based education.

Passage of the North Carolina Public School Law in 1839 offered state assistance for the provision of public schools in North Carolina counties. Davie County voted "for schools" on August 9, 1839, and by 1842, free schools operated in each of the 15 school districts established at the time.

Mocksville citizens voted in favor of construction of a "graded school" in 1907 to be financed by a $5,000 bond issue. The Mocksville Primary School on Cherry Street opened in 1911. In 1920, the standard school term increased from four to six months, from November through April. In that same year, the board of education encouraged school consolidation within districts and arranged for bus transportation for students in those districts that committed to building brick schools. The state assumed financial responsibility for public school operating expenses and increased the school term to eight months in the midst of the Great Depression in 1933. The State added the ninth month to the school term and the twelfth grade in 1943.

Mocksville High School opened on North Main Street in 1924 and operated until Davie High School opened in 1956, consolidating the four high schools in the county into one. The Brock Center now stands where Mocksville High School once stood.

Individuals, families, and organizations that influenced life in Mocksville share a chapter in this book; seek out someone you know. Growth and development in surrounding towns of Davie County mirrored development in the town of Mocksville, as seen in the last chapter.

As tantalizing as the photographs in this book may be to the viewer, even more tantalizing is the possibility of additional caches of old photographs in the possession of local residents who may not even realize the treasure troves they have. History comes alive as we rediscover and share old photographs and contemplate what they tell us of past times and lives. We hope you enjoy the history brought to light in this book.

One

TOWN OF MOCKSVILLE

TOWN OF MOCKSVILLE. The town of Mocksville originated from a village or mustering ground known as "Mocks Old Field," believed to have been named for Andrew Mock, who owned part of the land on which the town grew. The year of 1810 saw the establishment of a post office at Mocks Old Field, with the name changed to Mocksville between 1823 and 1826.

MOCKSVILLE TOWN SQUARE. Looking north up Main Street, the original courthouse stood in the center of the square facing south. Remnants of the old town well can be seen in front of the courthouse. C. C. Sanford Sons Company anchors the northwest corner on the left. On the right, the large porch on the building identifies the old Wiley Clement Store. Roy Holthouser gazes south from the rooftop.

DAVIE COUNTY COURTHOUSE. Davie County's first courthouse, opened in 1839, held court until 1909, when the new courthouse opened. The old building continued as a community center with space for a town hall, public library, and movie house. It was destroyed in 1922 to facilitate the paving of roads in Mocksville. In 1916, the ladies of the county succeeded in efforts to have a ladies restroom and lounge opened in the building. They requested that the gentlemen of the town refrain from smoking and spitting on the floor when passing through the hallway of the building. (Courtesy of Hugh S. Larew.)

COURTHOUSE SQUARE. Unidentified residents circle the old courthouse in their horse and buggy in the early 1900s. R. M. Meroney wrote about court week around the turn of the century in his This I Remember column of the *Davie Record* in 1955, saying, "The old court house would not hold the crowds that attended court in the old days. Wagons, buggies, carts, surreys, and hacks were used to bring folks to town. Horse traders had the back lots filled with horses and mules for sale. The patent medicine vendors were also on hand. Reuben Gaither, colored, with his barbecue, corn bread, and slaw fed all those who had a quarter on their person." (Courtesy of Lash and Cyrette Sanford.)

NORTHWEST CORNER OF THE SQUARE. Walter Clement poses in his buggy in front of Crawford's Drugstore and S. M. Call's store, likely in the 1920s based on the car parked in front of the store. (Courtesy of Lash and Cyrette Sanford.)

C. C. Sanford Sons Company. Calvin Cowles Sanford worked for Brown and Brothers Merchants in the mid-1860s until the Browns moved to Winston in 1867, at which time Sanford bought their store. Sanford later erected the brick building, around 1895, on the same site at the corner of Depot and Main Streets. The store operated for 102 years, closing in 1969. The photograph, possibly from the late 1880s, shows, from left to right, Rufus B. Sanford, unidentified, Ed Sanford, and C. C. Sanford. (Courtesy of Lash and Cyrette Sanford.)

C. C. Sanford Sons Interior. The store promised its customers "everything for everybody." (Courtesy of Lash and Cyrette Sanford.)

C. C. SANFORD SONS. The Harris-LeGrand Pharmacy (1925–1941 or 1942) can be seen in the right of the photograph. (Courtesy of Lash and Cyrette Sanford.)

C. C. SANFORD SONS SALE. Taken about 1920, this photograph shows C. C. Sanford Sons' store's sale on stoves, with Mocksville Drug Company and Crawford's Drugstore (1913–1925) in operation to the right. (Courtesy of Gwynn Meroney.)

MODERNIZED C. C. SANFORD STORE. C. C. Sanford Sons Company celebrated their 70th anniversary with a complete remodeling of the facade (above) and the interior (below) of the building in 1937. The store carried dry goods, clothing, shoes, cosmetics, notions, gifts, groceries, hardware, and appliances on the first floor. Furniture and plumbing supplies were on the second floor, and farm machinery and implements were available in the adjacent building. (Both, courtesy of Lash and Cyrette Sanford.)

MAIN STREET NORTHWEST CORNER OF THE SQUARE. Along the northwest corner of the square, a parade passes in front of Main Street businesses, including Mocksville Cash Store, Wallace Five and Ten, Hall's Drugstore, W. J. Johnson Department Store, and the Mocksville Hotel after its third story addition in 1935.

J. T. BAITY STORE BUILDING. John Thomas Baity constructed the Main Street building in 1905 on the site of the Yellow Stone House, an older frame commercial building. Baity operated a general store in the building until 1912. Dr. R. P. Anderson practiced dentistry on the second floor.

COURTHOUSE SQUARE, 1940s. A view of the square, photographed from the second floor of the courthouse during World War II, shows the oak trees planted in 1934. (Courtesy of Ray Tutterow.)

GREYHOUND BUS SERVICE. The Mocksville Greyhound Bus Station operated out of the Wilkins Drug Company from about 1930 until 1972, when it moved to Tutterow's Esso Service. Haines Yates, an employee of the drugstore, handled most of the bus service administrative work, and Henry Meroney greeted passengers. The drugstore maintained operating hours to coincide with the bus service. Bus drivers routinely came into the drugstore to "have a coke on the house." (Courtesy of Carol and Lisa LeGrand.)

RED FRONT BUILDING. In 1901, J. T. Baity came to Mocksville and opened a dry goods and notions store. Baity painted the front of the building red and called his store the Red Front. Roy Holthouser (left) and Armet Sheek pose in front of the building, which later housed the *Mocksville Enterprise*. (Courtesy of Gwynn Meroney.)

WEST DEPOT STREET. From left to right, an unidentified man, ? Clement, and Roy Holthouser pose in front of a McCormick combine. The old rental house pictured to the right stood on the site of the future Sanford Rankin Implement Company, and on the left are the backs of buildings on the northwest corner of the square. (Courtesy of Gwynn Meroney.)

SOUTHWEST SQUARE. The Bank of Davie, established in 1901, moved to the Masonic Building on the southwest side of the square in 1907. The bank merged with Branch Bank and Trust in 1967. The Masonic Building was demolished to make way for the Davie County Administration Building in 1984. The Sanford Brothers building appears to the right (above). (Left, courtesy of Lash and Cyrette Sanford.)

SANFORD BROTHERS BUILDING. Constructed in the 1920s for R. B. and J. C. Sanford, sons of Calvin Cowles Sanford, the Sanford Brothers building offered business and office space for rent. The Davie Café, owned and operated by P. K. Manos in the 1920s, occupied the front of the building. (Courtesy of Lash and Cyrette Sanford.)

DR. JOHN W. RODWELL (1865–1934). James H. Cain wrote the College of Physicians and Surgeons in Baltimore, Maryland, requesting a physician to practice in the Cana community in 1894. Dr. John William Rodwell accepted and relocated to Cana to practice general medicine. In 1904, Dr. Rodwell moved to Mocksville and opened a practice first in his home on Salisbury Street, then in a building on the site of Horn's Service Station, then in the Masonic Building, and lastly in the Sanford Building. The photograph shows Dr. Rodwell in his Sanford Building office during the 1920s. (Courtesy of Betty Etchison West.)

MOCKSVILLE POST OFFICE. The post office moved into the Sanford Building, next door to the Davie Café, in 1926. This 1934 photograph shows, from left to right, Daisy Holthouser (postmaster 1951), J. Arthur Daniel, Virginia Adams Waters, M. Boone Stonestreet, Armand T. Daniel, C. Spurgeon Anderson, and Samuel R. Latham.

PARKING METERS. Installed during the 1950s, parking meters in downtown Mocksville were met with the displeasure of both merchants and shoppers, leading eventually to their removal.

GASOLINE DELIVERY, C. 1939. Percy Brown (left) and Dick Everhart pose by their Essolube Motor Oil tanker during a delivery to Sanford Gas Station. The old M. D. Brown Livery Stable can be seen behind the truck, with the June Bailey Store building at the left in the background. (Courtesy of Gwynn Meroney.)

RANKIN SANFORD IMPLEMENT COMPANY. The implement company, located on the corner of Depot and North Clement Streets across from Sanford Motor Company, opened in 1945. The business, owned by David C. Rankin, John C. Sanford, and Rufus B. Sanford, sold International Harvester farm machinery and operated until 1966.

SANFORD MOTOR COMPANY. Calvin Cowles Sanford bought the lot known as the McNeely Store Lot or Old Factory Lot in 1901 and erected the Motor Company Building in 1916 to sell Fords, "the universal car." A touring model Ford, with one seat and curtains instead of windows, sold for $295 in 1924. The Town of Mocksville razed the building in 1977. (Courtesy of Lash and Cyrette Sanford.)

SANFORDS. From left to right, John Sanford, C. C. Sanford, Hugh Sanford, and Rufus B. Sanford pose in front of the Sanford Service Station. Rufus Brown Sanford rose to prominence in Mocksville with his family business interests and his longstanding involvement in the Masonic Lodge, including being treasurer for 25 years. He served as vice president and director of the Bank of Davie, charter member and past president of Mocksville Rotary Club, member of the Mocksville School Board from 1911 to 1947, and elder of First Presbyterian Church for 50 years. (Courtesy of Lash and Cyrette Sanford.)

MOCKSVILLE, AROUND 1900. Looking up North Main Street from the square, the businesses on the right have been identified as Wiley Clement's Store, later the Farmer's Alliance Store; a bar room in the little brick building, which later became a barber shop; the E. E. Hunt store; and the Gaither Tobacco Factory. On the left stand the Bill Bailey Store, the Frank Brown Store, and the J. T. Angell store. At the end of the unpaved street, the Gaither Law Office can be seen to the left. (Courtesy of the *Salisbury Post*.)

WILEY CLEMENT STORE BUILDING. The store building, with its wide porches, can be seen in the middle of the photograph. Wiley Clement ran a store in an old wooden building owned by E. L. Gaither. After the death of Captain Clement, a meat market opened in the building. When the meat market closed, a soda water bottling business rented the building. After the bottling business moved to Salisbury Street, Johnny Jones used the building as a place to buy poultry.

23

NORTHEAST SIDE OF THE SQUARE. Going down the block, the buildings include Jacob Stewart's law office; Horn's Service Station; the Horn Building; Gaither Tobacco Factory; E. E. Hunt Store, a small building that contained a bar room; and Wiley Clement's store. The courthouse is south of Depot Street. (Courtesy of Carol and Lisa LeGrand.)

WEANT BUILDING. Sheek's Barber Shop and Pool Room (right) operated in the old Weant Building at the time of this photograph. Note the Mayfair Beauty Shoppe sign. Jo Cooley (1915–1978) came to Mocksville in 1938 to operate the Mayfair Beauty Shoppe. Paralyzed from the waist down in an auto accident in 1942, Cooley continued to work in her shop full time until she sold it in 1972 and part time until her death in 1978. Cooley helped organize and served as the first president of the North Carolina Paraplegic Association. She worked tirelessly for the removal of architectural barriers for the handicapped. In recognition of her dedication, she received North Carolina's "Outstanding Handicapped Citizen of the Year" award in 1970. (Courtesy of Carol and Lisa LeGrand.)

SOUTHEAST SIDE OF THE SQUARE. The courthouse, built in 1909 and listed on the National Register of Historic Places in 1979, sits on the site of the old Kelly or Davie Hotel. (Courtesy of Carol and Lisa LeGrand.)

THOMAS E. DEWEY. Dewey, former governor of New York, paid a visit to Mocksville while campaigning for the presidency in 1948. The picture, taken on the steps of the courthouse, includes, from left to right, Wilburn F. Stonestreet, C. Frank Stroud, Nancy Tutterow, Charles R. Vogler, "Sol" Cook, state senator Burr Brock Sr., Katherine Hoots Reavis, Cecil Morris, and Inez Naylor Weaver. The passerby with the hat is unidentified. Harry S. Truman defeated Dewey in the election. (Courtesy of Ray Tutterow.)

TOWN SQUARE, 1932. This photograph, taken by Archie Holbrook from the courthouse steps, shows the town square prior to when the oak trees, which still exist today, were planted. A brass Gatling gun originally stood in the grass circle nearest the courthouse. Southern Bank and Trust Company operated in the large white building during the 1920s. Note the vacant lot to the left of the Mocksville Hotel in the northwest corner of the square. In 1934, the town supervisor, Hugh Lagle, and Ben Boyles drove out to a property along U.S. 158 and dug up four oak trees, which they then planted in the square. A plaque now commemorates their planting.

FOURTH OF JULY PARADE, 1940s. A parade advances north on Main Street, past the Masonic Building on the right and the courthouse, Southern Bank and Trust building, and American Café on the left.

OLD OFFICE BUILDING. The two story wooden building, believed to have been built by a Mr. Fitzgerald in the early 1800s, served as an office for attorney John Marshall Clement and his brother, Dr. Dewitt Clement. Dr. James McGuire and Dr. M. D. Kimbrough also occupied the building that stood south of the courthouse until 1951. The construction of the first Davie County Administration (now Office) Building led to the old office building's razing. Mocksville's second jail can be seen in the background, on the left in the photograph. (Courtesy of Lash and Cyrette Sanford.)

SOUTHEAST SQUARE. The old house in the photograph stood between the Davie County Office Building and the old jail before being torn down to construct the Mocksville Savings and Loan building.

DAVIE COUNTY JAIL. The National Register of Historic Places includes the old jail, built in 1839. Henry R. Austin, architect of the original courthouse, also designed the jail with jailers' living quarters on the first floor and cellblocks on the second floor. Used as a jail until 1909, Gaston E. Horn then converted the building to a private residence (above). Hugh S. Larew restored the building (below) in 1970.

WORLD WAR II BOND RALLY, 1944. Around 3,500 people attended Mocksville's fourth war loan bond rally on February 12, 1944. A parade, led by a 30-piece band from Camp Marshall and some field artillery, marched from the high school to the courthouse. Knox Johnstone, county chairman of the War Finance committee, presented a captured German helmet to the William R. Davie School for the best war slogan banner: "Hit 'em hard, hit 'em fast; win the peace, make it last." Huge crowds lined the Yadkinville Highway to see 26 paratroopers jumping from a plane at Woodruff Farm. Twelve bombers flew over the town and dropped leaflets urging everyone to buy war bonds. Unfortunately, high winds carried the leaflets several blocks from the square. The event sold over $17,000 in war bonds.

NATIONAL GUARD. With 49 original members, the Davie County National Guard Medical Company formed in February 1947 and received its charter on September 29, 1947. Dr. William M. Long served as the first commander until being honorably discharged in 1951. Dr. Lester P. Martin Sr. and his wife, Helen Bahnson Martin, donated land for construction of the unit's first armory, with a provision that the title would revert to the Martins when the National Guard no longer needed the property. A new armory was constructed in the early 1970s. The unit parades down Main Street in the photograph. (Courtesy of Carol and Lisa LeGrand.)

ARMISTICE DAY, 1951. The last full scale Armistice Day celebration held in Mocksville on November 11, 1951, drew an estimated crowd of 2,500. Red, white, and blue flags and bunting bedecked downtown Mocksville. In the photograph, Robert S. McNeill, the master of ceremonies, is introducing the program. Ray Calloway, former state commander of the American Legion, delivered the principal address on the Korean conflict. The program featured speeches, music, and recognition of Gold Star Mothers. Armistice Day, designated to commemorate the end of hostilities between World War I allies and Germany, became known as Veterans Day in the United States after World War II.

CIVILIAN CONSERVATION CORPS (CCC). The CCC, established in 1933, provided public relief and vocational training designed to relieve unemployment during the Great Depression. The photograph captures a Smith family visit to the CCC camp near Elkin, North Carolina, and includes, from left to right, (first row) Julie Smith, Dot Smith, Eva Mae Smith, and George Smith; (second row) Mary S. Smith, Mattie Mabe, Bud Smith, Iris Hepler, and Grant Smith. Grant and Bud Smith worked at the camp prior to entering military service. The Mocksville CCC camp on Wilkesboro Street operated for about two years in the early 1940s. Lester P. Martin Jr. played the trumpet in the Mocksville CCC Band. (Courtesy of Estelle Smith.)

PAVING THE STREETS. A paving machine moves alongside the horses and buggies on North Main Street near the First United Methodist Church in 1922. Located behind the trees, Mary Heitman's home stood across the street. In 1921, Depot Street became the first road in the county to be paved. (Courtesy of Carol and Lisa LeGrand.)

North Main Street, Mocksville, N. C.

NORTH MAIN STREET, 1924. A Model T car travels north on Main Street, passing Spring Street and the Casey and Stonestreet General Store on the left. Built in 1903, John D. Casey, and later his brother Oscar Casey, ran the store. In 1948, Otis Hendrix purchased and operated the store until 1973.

CARTER MEDICAL OR GAITHER LAW OFFICE BUILDING. Archibald G. Carter constructed this building as a medical office for his son, Dr. Jesse Carter, in the late 1840s or early 1850s. The building stood on the corner of North Main and Gaither Streets. In the late 1870s, Dr. James McGuire rented the building for his medical practice. Ephraim Gaither bought the property in 1884. Gaither's son E. L. Gaither used the building for a law office, as did his grandson R. B. Sanford Jr. In 1967, Sanford sold the lot to Knox Johnstone and moved the building to its present site on North Main Street. The photograph below shows the interior of the law office. (Both, courtesy of Lash and Cyrette Sanford.)

MACK D. BROWN FARM. The Brown Farm stood at the site of the current Ingersoll-Rand Plant. Kathryn Brown, Clayton Brown, and Meek A. Brown deeded their farmland to Masland Duraleather Company in 1960, which subsequently deeded it to Ingersoll-Rand in 1968. Mack Brown carried the mail from the depot with his horse and wagon. (Courtesy of Lash and Cyrette Sanford.)

PASS STORE BUILDING. Richard Pass built the store on Depot Street for a man who helped him on his farm in the early 1900s. The building represents numerous early two-story frame commercial structures, which were later replaced by brick structures.

MOCKSVILLE CHAIR FACTORY. Gaston Horn organized the Mocksville Chair Company, which began operation in 1901, and served as its superintendent and general manager. The plant, located at Salisbury and West Maple Streets in the old Brown Brothers Tobacco Factory, turned out thousands of chairs and provided employment to a number of Mocksville citizens. The factory bought 4-foot oak logs, cut out the chair from the raw material, and used the waste part of the wood to fire the boilers for steam power. The company dissolved in 1917, and all property and machinery sold at auction. The photographer stood in the yard of the old Meroney Home.

MOCKSVILLE CHAIR FACTORY WORKERS. W. H. Smith is the fourth man from the left on the second row. All others are unidentified.

HANES CHAIR AND FURNITURE COMPANY. Until its bankruptcy in 1960, the Hanes Chair and Furniture Company ranked as one of the oldest names in the furniture business. J. B. Johnstone and J. F. Hanes formed the Hanes Chair and Table Company in the late 1890s or early 1900s. In 1937, they sold the company to R. D. Bayliss and J. W. Harris, who continued operation as the Hanes Chair and Novelty Company. In 1947, Don Headen purchased the company and incorporated as Hanes Chair and Furniture Company. The company manufactured commercial office furniture, institutional equipment, and household items.

W. G. WHITE AND COMPANY. William Green White opened W. G. White and Company in November of 1924 as a general merchandise and country produce store, located on Cherry Street in Winston-Salem. William's good friend and former employee at W. C. White and Company in Advance, W. G. "Major" Shermer, moved his family to Winston-Salem and worked in the store. The company runs a ham processing shop and small country-retail store in Davie County today. These photographs show the store in Winston-Salem. W. G. White stands second from the right (above), and Will Shermer is third from the right. In the photograph below, Will Shermer also appears on the right. (Both, courtesy of Robert Stafford.)

MO-DA-NO-CA HUNTING LODGE. Built around 1920 and owned by Walter Clement, the lodge featured pine-log construction, big open fireplaces, and a comfortable porch. Located three blocks west of the square on Avon Street, it contained 11 rooms. Clement held a contest to name the lodge and offered a prize of $5. Frank Stroud's entry won. Mo-Da-No-Ca stands for Mocksville, Davie, and North Carolina. The lodge burned down a few years after opening.

BOGER OIL COMPANY. Dr. R. P. Anderson built the service station, one of the oldest in Mocksville, in 1920 and sold it to Pure Oil Company in 1931. Albert Boger became a partner in the station with Grady Ward in 1946, operating as Boger and Ward Service. Sam Howard later bought Ward's share of the business, and the station operated as Boger and Howard. The station became Boger Pure Service in 1954. Albert Denton Boger purchased the property from the Pure Oil Company in 1965, and the Boger brothers expanded the business into a fuel oil distribution company. The photograph dates to around 1951. (Courtesy of Dean Allen.)

RAILROAD DEPOT. A new brick train depot replaced the old depot building in 1980. The old depot, erected in 1891, was donated to the Davie County Historical Museum committee and moved 100 yards down the street to the former location of the old ice plant. Plans included renovation of the building to become part of a proposed Davie County Historical Museum complex located adjacent to the Masonic picnic grounds. Those renovations never occurred, and the building gradually fell into decay and no longer exists.

MOVING THE DEPOT. Crouch Moving Company of Salisbury required eight hours to move the old depot to the new location 100 yards down the street. Tree limbs, phone lines, and electrical lines had to be cut to permit relocation of the building.

DAVIE FURNITURE COMPANY. The 1956 annual meeting of the Davie Electric Membership Corporation includes a demonstration of the Siegler soot-free heater. W. J. B. Sell, owner of Davie Furniture Company, an authorized Siegler dealer, stands on the right.

SHUTT AND BOWDEN FIRESTONE STORE. George Henry Clay Shutt operated the Firestone store that was located on Main Street. Shutt served for 27 years on the Davie County Board of Education. He also served as Mocksville town clerk, registrar of deeds, treasurer, accountant, and tax collector. Shutt, an avid cigar smoker, collected cigar bands to exchange for premiums. When his wife, Virginia Poe Shutt, began to use the cigar bands to order things other than the socks that Shutt originally started saving them for, Sen. B. Everett Jordan, whom Shutt served as 1972 Davie County campaign manager, sent him two pairs of socks. The senator said he knew that in a showdown between Shutt and his wife over the cigar bands, it would be Shutt on the losing end.

HENDRICKS AND MERRELL FURNITURE. Clyde Hendricks (left) and Bill Merrell pick up a load of furniture at the Mocksville Train Depot. The Mocksville Feed Mill can be seen in the background

DAVIE RECORD. Founded by E. H. Morris, the first copy of the *Davie Record* was printed on April 1, 1899. Morris sold the newspaper to C. Frank Stroud on November 27, 1908. Stroud published the newspaper for 49 years. The *Davie Record* merged with the *Mocksville Enterprise* in 1957. The photograph shows C. Frank Stroud and Julia Marmaduke "Duke" Sheek, the printer's devil, setting the lead letters by hand in the newspaper offices.

UNDER THE ARBOR. The newspaper archives identified the photograph as the Masonic Picnic; however, local historians agree that the picture does not portray the Masonic Picnic Arbor. After eliminating Center Arbor as a possibility, the possibility exists that the picture may have been taken at the old Baptist Arbor, which stood off of North Main Street near the end of town. It had the capacity to seat 2,000 people. The Baptist Arbor hosted the annual Sunday School and Orphanage Picnic to benefit the Thomasville Orphanage from 1891 to 1905. In 1906, the arbor was dismantled and moved to Thomasville to be rebuilt on the grounds of the Mills Home. A letter from Mrs. E. Frost, written in 1892, talks about the two picnics held in Mocksville, stating, "the Masonic Picnic was much larger in number and wickedness. No drinking at the Orphanage (picnic), but at the Masonic they were fighting before twelve." Sunnyside Academy also held commencement ceremonies at the Baptist Arbor. (Courtesy of the *Salisbury Post*.)

MOCKSVILLE MASONIC PICNIC. The Masonic Picnic, held in Mocksville since 1883, benefits the Masonic Orphanage of Oxford. For many years, speakers and orphans sat on a small, wooden platform. The crowd sat on benches without backs, and no roof existed, only the branches of oak trees. Long tables under the trees held the picnic dinner. The first arbor, erected in 1899, remained in use until it burned in 1958. Around 1892, the first excursion train ran from Winston to the picnic. By the early 1900s, the fame of the picnic had spread beyond the borders of the state. (Courtesy of Hugh S. Larew.)

LAKE HIDE-AWAY. The lake, located off of Highway 158, opened in 1954 and became one of the most popular social spots in Mocksville. In addition to the white sand beach, the resort included a bathhouse, concession stand, a lounge with jukebox, and a miniature golf course. (Both, courtesy of Carol and Lisa LeGrand.)

RICH PARK. Baseball reigned as a very popular sport all through the county and provided live entertainment before the days of radio and television. The town's semiprofessional team and high school team used an old baseball field on Milling Road until after World War II, when the American Legion built a new field at Rich Park. The Mocksville Millers baseball team then entered the Yadkin Valley League. Community baseball flourished as well, which was before Little League came into vogue. At a 1992 reunion, veterans of community baseball talked about having to plow fields before going to play ball, wearing overalls or whatever they had, and having to look for the baseball if someone hit it long. (Courtesy of Carol and Lisa LeGrand.)

MISS MOCKSVILLE OF 1965. Marsha Stewart of Cooleemee receives her crown from Miss Mocksville of 1964, Dottie Howard. From left to right are Sue Crotts, Miss Congeniality; Sherry Collins, second runner-up; Dottie Howard, who is crowning Marsha Stewart; and Dianne Hendricks, first runner-up.

CHRISTMAS PARADE. Floats line up for a Christmas parade in front of the old Mocksville High School.

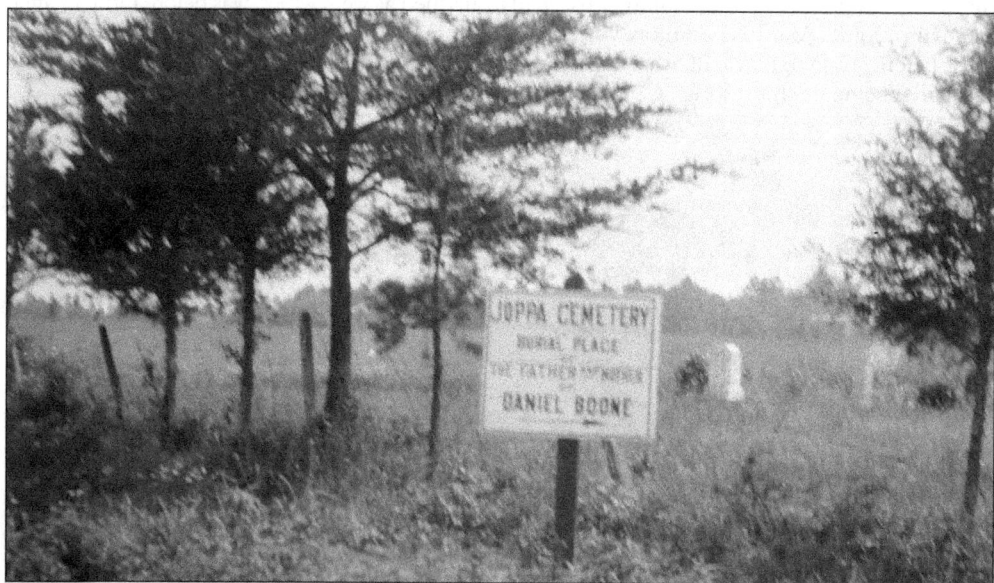

JOPPA CEMETERY. The cemetery, originally known as Burying Ground Ridge, holds the graves of Daniel Boone's parents, Squire and Sarah, and his brother, Israel. Israel's grave predates that of his father, long thought to be the oldest in the cemetery. Israel died of tuberculosis in 1756 after having received treatment from the Moravian settlement in Salem. A memorial for Israel, placed in May 2009, now marks his approximate burial site. An interdenominational meetinghouse, Forks of the Yadkin, was erected on the site in 1767. The congregation requested a minister from the Presbyterian Synod. In 1789, the Presbyterian General Assembly changed the church name to Joppa, a biblical term meaning beauty. The cemetery name likely changed at the same time. (Courtesy of Carol and Lisa LeGrand.)

FIRST PRESBYTERIAN CHURCH OF MOCKSVILLE. Organized in 1767 as the Forks of the Yadkin Meetinghouse, the church later became Joppa Presbyterian Church and then First Presbyterian Church. The original meetinghouse stood at Joppa Cemetery. About 1835, the church moved to a temporary location on Salisbury Street in Mocksville. A brick sanctuary was erected in 1840 on Main Street. The present church followed in 1905. (Courtesy of Hugh S. Larew.)

FIRST PRESBYTERIAN MANSE. The manse, built in 1890, stood on South Main Street beside the Presbyterian Church. Both Dr. W. C. Martin and Dr. J. W. Rodwell rented the manse from the church at one time. A new manse replaced the original manse in 1951. (Courtesy of Hugh S. Larew.)

METHODIST CHURCH, Mocksville, N. C.

FIRST UNITED METHODIST CHURCH. Letitia Carter, wife of Archibald Carter, donated the land for the first church. Jesse Clement furnished most of the lumber. The church stood at the site of the present Mocksville Police Department and featured a white, wooden frame with steps leading up to two front doors. The interior included a balcony that was used for African American slaves. The balcony was removed after the Civil War. Church members erected the brick church in 1895 and dedicated it in August 1896.

REV. WILLIAM C. WILLSON (C. 1835–1903). Willson served as a second lieutenant for Company F, North Carolina 42nd Regiment, during the Civil War. After the war, he joined the Methodist Conference at Greensboro in 1867. He was the pastor for a group of churches in Davie County, including First United Methodist in 1887, and lived in the parsonage on Salisbury Street. A Mason, he spoke at the 1892 Masonic Picnic. Willson also served on the board of the North Carolina Midlands Railroad. His wife, Alice Long Willson, raised silkworms. As children in the Willson's neighborhood, Martha Call and Frances Morris gathered mulberry leaves to feed the silkworms.

FIRST BAPTIST CHURCH. Construction of the First Baptist Church sanctuary occurred around 1918. Members of the building committee included L. G. Horn, G. E. Horn, Jacob Stewart, John Minor, and Dr. W. C. Martin. In 1966, the church decided to tear down this sanctuary and construct the sanctuary that exists today. (Courtesy of Carol and Lisa LeGrand.)

SUNDAY SCHOOL CLASS, c. 1920. C. Frank Stroud's Sunday school class poses on the steps of the First Baptist Church on North Main Street in Mocksville. From left to right stand (first row) Eva Call, Mary Campbell, and Virginia Reece; (second row) Hilia Smith, Mabel Stewart, C. F. Stroud Sr., Mary Horn, and Audrey Brenegar.

SHILOH BAPTIST CHURCH CONGREGATION. The church organized in 1885 in the home of Calvin and Mary Bryant. A new brick church erected on another Depot Street lot in 1934 replaced the original wooden church building, located on the south side of Depot Street. Rev. Wise Hairston served as the first pastor until 1915.

SHILOH SUNDAY SCHOOL. The 1951 Sunday school class at Shiloh Baptist Church includes (first row) George Hairston, George Smith, Rev. George W. Campbell, and Minnie Groce Campbell; (second row) Elizabeth Mason Johnson, Alice Hudson Anderson Britton, Seresa Britton Mason, Alva Cain Crawford, and Lillian Britton Cain.

Two

PASSING PARADE

McNeely-Weant House. Built in the early 1830s by Thomas McNeely, the house, one of Mocksville's oldest, stood for more than 100 years. The large, two-story structure with twin chimneys on the north side featured rooms of unusual dimensions. The walls were painted yellow and had high wainscoting that was painted red, green, and yellow. The mantels were painted in a granite pattern of green and yellow with a border design of grapes and leaves. The treads of the stairway had carved ornaments, and the banister rail was of walnut or mahogany with curved newel posts. The front door, with its high stone steps, faced Salisbury Street. At that time, Salisbury Street was the main thoroughfare in town. Paved with bricks, a deep piazza lined the east side. In the early 1900s, the structure served as the home of W. A. Weant and his sisters. W. A. Weant, a veteran tinsmith, had the distinction of making his own coffin of intricate tin workmanship several years before his death.

THOMAS BROWN HOUSE. The home, located on Salisbury Street, was believed to have been built in 1800 by Cannon Brown. Thomas and Margaret (Brinegar) Brown occupied the house soon after their marriage in 1829. The town condemned and demolished the house in 1971. When the outer boards were removed from the home, workers found that the original house consisted of a simple two-story structure that measured 21-by-17 feet. Typical of the early period, the original house had one room downstairs and one upstairs.

THOMAS BROWN (1807–1881).
Brown married Margaret Brinegar
(1809–1876), daughter of Joshua and
Sarah Brinegar. Brown served as a
trustee of the old Joppa Church. He
became a deacon in 1841 and an elder
in 1853. William and Rufus Brown,
two sons of Thomas Brown, operated
the Brown Brothers Mercantile Store,
which was later sold to C. C. Sanford.
They also ran a tobacco factory on
Salisbury Street, which moved to
Winston-Salem in 1877. By 1878,
Brown Brothers Tobacco ranked as
the largest tobacco manufacturer
in Winston-Salem and later merged
with the R. J. Reynolds Company.

DR. BAXTER CLEGG CLEMENT (1841–1886). Clement, the sixth child of Jesse A. and Malinda Clement, was born in Mocksville. During the Civil War, Clement served as captain of Company M, North Carolina 7th Regiment, Confederate Cavalry. After the war, Clement apprenticed with his brother Dr. William Clement and later attended the University of Louisiana for further medical training. He practiced medicine with his brother in Arkansas before returning to Rowan County, North Carolina, in 1880. Around 1883, he married Lina Barber and moved back to Mocksville, which was where he lived until his death. (Courtesy of Carol and Lisa LeGrand.)

JESSE CLEMENT HOUSE BEFORE RESTORATION. Jesse A. Clement built the plantation house around 1828, which makes it one of the oldest homes in the county. A prominent farmer and politician in Mocksville, Clement operated a tannery, two plantations, and a brokerage firm that dealt in manufactured plug tobacco, cotton, and wheat. During the Civil War, Clement commanded the Davie Grays, Company F, North Carolina 13th Regiment.

DESCENDENTS OF CLEMENT SLAVES, 1978. Shown in front of the Jesse Clement House before the restoration are, from left to right, William Eugene Gaither, Ruth Clement Bond, Dr. Abbie Clement Jackson, Jane Clement Howard-Bond, and Magdalene Dulin Gaither.

JESSE CLEMENT HOUSE AFTER RESTORATION. In February 1978, the Historic Preservation Fund of North Carolina took an option to purchase the home in hopes of finding a new owner who would restore the property. Rev. William F. Long, pastor of the First Presbyterian Church in Mocksville from 1958 to 1962, purchased the home later in 1978 from the Clement heirs and restored it to its original condition. The National Park Service listed the house on the National Register of Historic Places in 1979.

HOWELL HOUSE. The Salisbury Street house dates to around 1830. The first known owner was Stephen L. Howell, a merchant in business with Thomas McNeely. Howell served as Registrar of Deeds of Davie County. Howell had eight children, three of whom died in November and December of 1862. The three lie buried in the yard to the rear of the house. The northern part of the house predates the southern part, which was added during the 1860s. The house features large brick chimneys constructed of handmade bricks and wide, pine board floors. In 1863, the property was deeded to W. L. Brown, and the above picture was made during his ownership of the home, probably around 1875. The home sold in 1880 to C. C. Sanford. The Larew family lived in the home in later years. The original small brick Mocksville Academy building, chartered *c.* 1825, stands in the yard.

LAREW CHILDREN. From left to right, Frank Larew, Hugh Larew, and John Larew Jr. pose with an unidentified friend on his pony in front of the family's Packard automobile. (Courtesy of Hugh S. Larew.)

McGUIRE HOUSE. Dr. James McGuire sits in front of the house he built on North Main Street around 1880. The home, last occupied by A. T. Grant, was torn down during the early summer of 1965. R. S. Meroney reminisced about Dr. McGuire in a 1954 newspaper column that was entitled This I Remember. He said, "Dr. McGuire was really one of the old-time doctors and wore conventional clothing of early colonial days. I can still see Dr. McGuire in his long-tail coat, high silk hat, and high top boots, on the top of which was stamped the head of a horse and riding whip, which I thought were about the prettiest footwear in the world."

PEARSON HOUSE BEFORE RESTORATION. Jesse A. Pearson, a son of Richmond Pearson, built the home prior to 1823. Pearson lived in Rowan County prior to 1815, when he returned to Mocksville with his second wife, Elizabeth Wilson, and occupied The Oaks, a plantation south of Mocksville that was part of his wife's dowry. At this time, the house on Salisbury Street was built.

ANNIE GRANT'S HAT SHOP AND GRANT HOUSE. Rebecca Parker Grant, wife of Absalom Turner Grant Sr. and Annie's mother, bought the house from Louisa C. Moss in 1891. The home stood on the west side of North Main Street at Cherry Street. "Miss Annie's" hat shop occupied an added room on the north side of the house. The newspaper announcement of the shop opening stated, "To my many friends in Mocksville and Davie County, it is with pleasure that I announce my millinery opening, which is to take place on March 24, 1916. It is needless to say that I will show everything that could be procured in the most up-to-date styles in millinery and trimmings and I have supplemented my line very largely this season with some beautiful dress fabrics, as well as new silk novelties." Anne Parker Grant lived from 1866 to 1944.

EATON HOUSE. Blanche, Mattie, and Joseph Eaton, the daughters and son of Jacob and Mary Clement Eaton, lived in the Gaither Street house, built in 1892. Mattie Eaton began teaching school at the age of 15 with her father at Clay Hill Seminary, located near the present Davie County High School. She taught in or near Mocksville for 42 years. The home was torn down in 1972.

BELL HOUSE. Possibly built by Giles Pearson, the Bell House stood on Salisbury Street. In 1853, John Marshall Clement and his bride, Mary Jane Hayden Clement, moved into the house and lived there for seven years. Later the Adams family lived in the house. After the death of James Adams, his wife, Amanda, married Dr. Marshall Bell. When Dr. Bell built another house on Salisbury Street, the home was sold to W. L. Sanford. John Sanford owned the home when it burned in 1975.

JOHN MARSHALL CLEMENT (1825–1886). One of Clement's first teachers in Mocksville was Peter Ney (thought by some to be Napoleon's Marshal Ney). Later in life, Clement recalled the scar across Ney's forehead and the fencing lessons he taught to the students using canes cut from the forest. At the age of 16, Clement entered Hugh Hill at Bethany in Iredell County. Afterward, he attended Rev. Baxter Clegg's school and Mocksville Academy. In 1844, he entered Pennsylvania College at Gettysburg and remained there for two years. Clement returned to Mocksville in 1846, studied law at Richmond Hill, and was admitted to the bar in 1848. After spending one term in the state legislature, he devoted the rest of his life to the practice of law. In his later years, he refused to appear for the prosecution in cases where a life was at stake. (Courtesy of Lash and Cyrette Sanford.)

GRANT DANIEL HOUSE. The house stood at the corner of South Main and Water Streets until it was demolished in the 1960s to build a bank on the site. The home had been owned and occupied over the years by the following: Rev. P. H. Dalton, who built the house; T. J. Byerly; Ellen Powers Lemmie and Nannie Powers (daughters of sculptor Hiram Powers); Grant Daniel; and Hugh Larew. (Courtesy of Hugh S. Larew.)

FAMILY OF HIRAM POWERS. Hiram Powers, a renowned American sculptor, moved his family to Italy in the 1800s. Nannie Powers (on the far right in the second row, behind her father) and Ellen Powers (seated beside her father) moved to Mocksville in 1914 and lived in the Grant Daniel House, the Meroney House, and finally the old Brown House. They erected a building in the backyard of the Brown House for their cats, with a runway to the second story of the house for the cats' convenience. Nannie Powers lies buried in Joppa Cemetery.

ABRAHAM M. NAIL HOUSE. The house, located on Main Street, was built in the 1880s for Abraham M. Nail (1854–1896) and his wife, Ida Rose Nail (1851–1946). Nail designed and built the unusual home himself. The home boasted Mocksville's first doorbell. Family friends and strangers came to the front door for no other reason than to ring the doorbell. Nail worked as a manager with the Forepaugh Circus and traveled with his sister, Mariah Nail Mertz.

MARRIAGE OF MARIAH NAIL AND JOHN MERTZ. Nail, a native of Mocksville, married Mertz in Louisville, Kentucky, on August 16, 1883. After traveling for many years with the circus, Mertz reportedly asked Nail if she would like to become engaged and travel together. The clerk of court asked the couple if they were old enough to get married, due to their small size, when they applied for their marriage license. Their marriage occurred on stage at the Buckingham Theatre before a large number of spectators. At 9:00 p.m. the curtain rose, disclosing a stage set in the style of a fashionable drawing room. The couple stood under a large floral bell suspended from the proscenium. The orchestra played a lively march. Julia Walcott and the San Francisco Quartet sang "Marriage Bells." The bride wore a dress of white satin with a long white veil interwoven with orange blossoms, fourteen-button white kid gloves, and satin slippers in a child's size six. The couple spent their honeymoon in Louisville.

NAIL-BROWN HOUSE.
A. M. and Ida Rose
Nail bought the house
from S. S. Nail in the
1880s. Percy Brown
bought the house from
A. M. Nail Jr. in 1921.
The house, located on
North Main Street,
was burned in 2009.

JOHN MERTZ (1853–1938). Maj. John
Mertz poses with Salisbury police chief
Lee Rankin. Mertz was named an
honorary policeman of Salisbury and
wore his policeman's uniform when
performing his functionary duty as
outer guard for the Knights of Pythias.
(Courtesy of the *Salisbury Post*.)

LOG HOUSE. Phineas Bailey and his wife, Josephine B. Bailey, occupied the house located on Salisbury Street and Sanford Avenue. The older, northern end of the house featured log construction. The southern end of the house was post and beam construction. The house was demolished in the 1990s. (Courtesy of the *Salisbury Post*.)

PHINEAS M. BAILEY (1835–1899). Bailey served as the mayor of Mocksville and was elected county coroner in 1898. His wife, Josephine Bailey, cooked for the Ingleside Lodge. (Courtesy of Gwynn Meroney.)

RICHMOND PEARSON HOME. Judge Richmond Pearson built the home in the early 1800s. After Pearson relocated to Yadkin County, other occupants of the home included Eliza Pearson Beatty, Thomas Gaither, Abner Kelly, William Jones, and Frank Brown. The home operated as Ingleside Hunting Lodge around 1900, catering to sportsmen from the North during quail shooting season. In 1902, the Johnstone family purchased the house. The home, which stood at North Main and Gaither Streets, was demolished by Knox Johnstone to build the Bank of Davie, which merged with Branch Banking and Trust in 1967.

JUNIUS BAILEY (1852–1912). Junius Bailey, the operator of Ingleside Hunting Lodge, sits alongside his wife, Sophronia Meroney Bailey (1843–1924). He also owned the June Bailey Store, which was located on the corner of Clement and Water Streets. (Courtesy of Gwynn Meroney.)

LEE HOUSE. Braxton Bailey built the home in 1838. In 1865, Gen. George Stoneman and his raiders stopped at the house. When angered by Jane McEwen Johnstone Bailey's repeated answers that she had no money hidden in the house, the soldiers put a pistol to her temple and set fire to a pillow on the bed. The soldiers left without harming her before the fire spread. The fire was extinguished after burning only a small place on the wall. The history room of the Davie County Public Library houses the burnt board. Later the home of Alice, Bertha, and Mary Lee, the house no longer stands.

Residence of Dr. R. P. Anderson, Main St., Mocksville, N. C.

DR. R. P. ANDERSON HOUSE. Barber and Kluttz of Knoxville, Tennessee, designed the house, built in 1903. Dr. Anderson, born in 1868 in the Calahaln community, graduated from the School of Dentistry at Vanderbilt University in 1890 and practiced dentistry in Mocksville until his retirement in 1958. (Courtesy of Jack Pennington.)

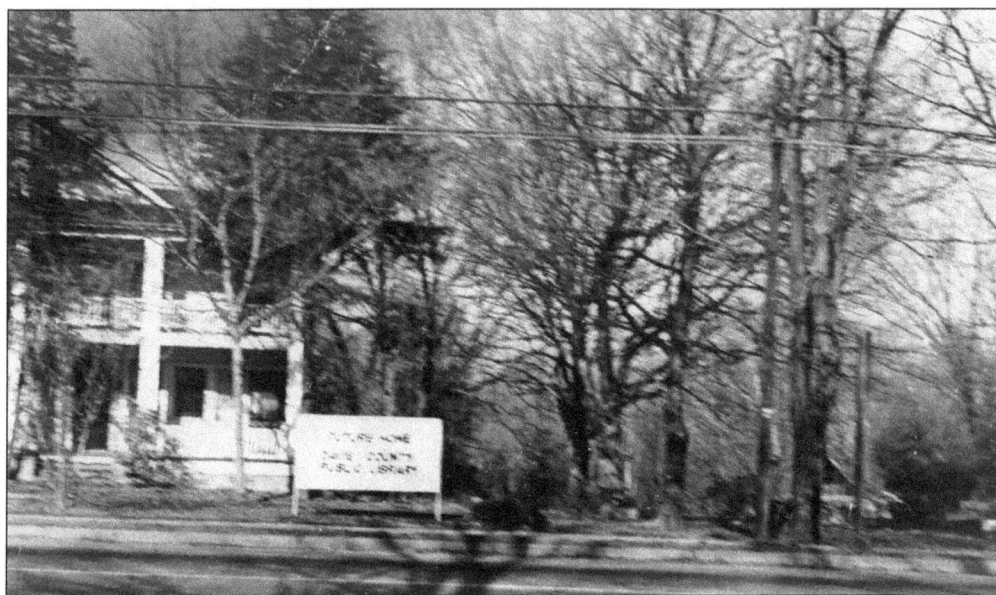

DODD HOUSE. The former home of Rev. Walter and Leonora Taylor Dodd was demolished in the mid-1960s for construction of the Davie County Public Library. Born in Clayton, North Carolina, in 1872, Dodd served as a Baptist minister for 30 years in various places around the state, including Mocksville Baptist. He was a member of the Masonic Lodge and died in 1950. A native of Mocksville, Leonora Dodd taught school locally and became principal of Mocksville Academy. She died in 1958.

LIBRARY BOARD OF TRUSTEES. Trustees who dedicated the new library in April 1966 include, from left to right, H. R. Hendrix, Knox Johnstone, Wyona Merrill Johnson, Ruth Bowman, Roy Huffner, John M. Groce, and George Henry Clay Shutt.

GRANT HOUSE. The home of Absalom Turner Grant Jr. was sold to the First Baptist Church at his death and torn down in 1965. The lot, adjacent to the Library, now provides parking.

ABSALOM TURNER GRANT JR. (1876–1962). Grant, born in Davie County, graduated from the University of North Carolina and was licensed to practice law in 1900. He practiced in Mocksville until his death in 1962 and served as county attorney for 29 terms. He was elected the first counselor of the North Carolina State Bar and served for six years. He represented Davie County in the North Carolina House of Representatives for six years between 1903 and 1927. He served three years in the North Carolina Senate. The January 14, 1931, *Davie Record* reported, "Senator A. T. Grant, Davie County Republican, held a caucus with himself and after some disagreement named himself minority floor leader. Grant, with Roy A. Hartman, Avery County, comprises the Republican delegation in the Senate. 'At first it was hard to reach an agreement,' Grant remarked humorously." During his last years, he served as judge of the Davie County Civil Court.

Jacob Stewart Home. The house stood on North Main Street at the site of the Church of Christ and was demolished around 1957.

Jacob "Colonel" Stewart (1860–1956). Colonel Stewart opened his law office on the square in Mocksville in 1888. He served as the attorney for the Davie County Board of Education, attorney for the Town of Mocksville, chairman of the Mocksville School Board, chairman of the annual Masonic Picnic, and a trustee of the First Baptist Church. When ready to go home from a day's work, Stewart picked up the telephone, and when the operator said "Number Please," he replied "Jitney" and hung up the phone. The town operator then called a cab and told the driver to pick up Stewart at his office and drive him home.

CALL ANDERSON HOUSE. James A. Call built the house in the mid-1890s. In 1898, the house was sold to Zolliecoffer and Jennie Anderson. After their deaths, the house passed to their daughter Mary Anderson Slye. Note that Main Street remains unpaved at the time of the photograph. (Courtesy of Taylor Slye.)

MUMFORD HOUSE. The house, built by Giles Mumford around 1812, stood at Mumford and Wilkesboro Streets. After the death of one of the Mumford children, the child's casket was lost off of the back of the wagon carrying it to Salisbury for burial. Considered to be haunted, the home no longer exists. Giles Mumford reported in 1877 that as a student, he used to deliver Peter Stuart Ney's mail. Ney read the *Carolina Watchman* first since he frequently contributed articles to the paper. Upon reading of the death of Napoleon's son, Mumford wrote that Ney "became deathly pale, rose from his desk, threw the paper to the floor, jumped on it, and stamped it to pieces, then said, 'Now damn you, lie there!'"

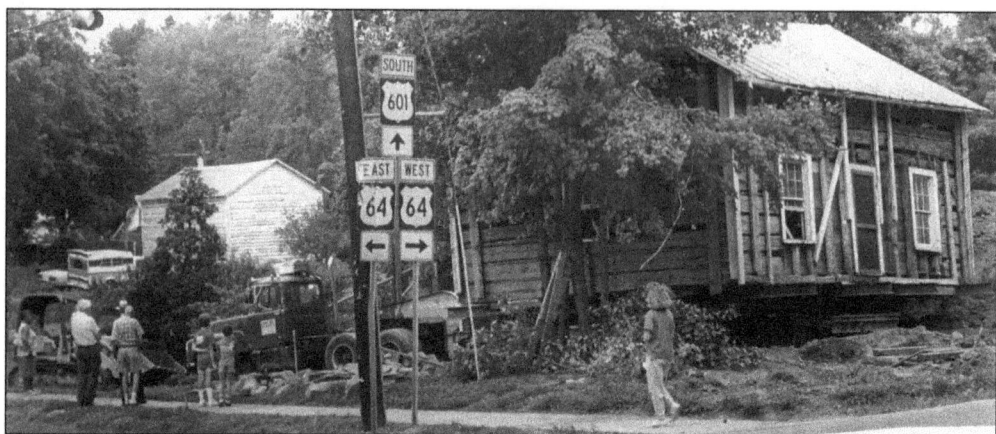

FROST CABIN. The cabin at the corner of South Main Street and Lexington Road was moved and restored in 1988 by Hugh S. Larew. Henry Darr of Davidson County purchased property in Mocksville for his two illegitimate daughters by a Cherokee Indian woman. The small cabin, built before 1840, passed down through the family for many years until Larew purchased the home from descendants of the daughters. (Courtesy of Hugh S. Larew.)

HENRY R. CALL HOUSE. Built by Jim Call, son of Henry R. Call, the little room on the left side of the house boasted the first bathroom built in Mocksville. Call placed a barrel on top of the bathroom and installed a large bathtub in the room. Every morning, he drew buckets of water from the well, climbed a ladder to the roof, and filled the barrel. During the day, the sun warmed the water and Call would come home from work in the evening to a hot bath. Curious people came from all over the county to view the bathroom and bathtub.

Three

SCHOOL DAYS

COMMENCEMENT PARADE. The school commencement parade passes the southwest side of the square. The Swicegood Hotel can be seen at the right in the background of the picture. The house in the background of the photograph (left) stood on the corner of South Main and Water Streets. (Courtesy of Carol and Lisa LeGrand.)

PETER STUART NEY (?–1846). A native of France, Ney arrived in Charleston, South Carolina, in 1816 and taught school in Davie, Iredell, and Rowan Counties from about 1823 to his death. He was buried in Rowan County in 1846. Considered a fine scholar and strict teacher, his students both feared and revered him. At times, Ney claimed to be Marshal Michel Ney, Napoleon's "bravest of the brave." He possessed precise military knowledge and a bearing that lent credence to his claims. He showed extreme distress at the death of Napoleon's only son in 1832. Allegedly, on his deathbed, Peter Stuart Ney confessed to being Marshal Ney. Debate as to his true identity continues today. (Courtesy of Davidson College Archives.)

MOCKSVILLE ACADEMY. On February 12, 1827, the North Carolina General Assembly chartered the Mocksville Academy. Trustees of the newly chartered school, Thomas McNeely, James F. Martin, William F. Kelly, A. G. Carter, A. R. Jones, and Richmond Pearson, built the building, located on Salisbury Street. Peter Stuart Ney taught at the academy.

JOHN ALEXANDER MERONEY HOUSE. Meroney moved to Mocksville around 1820 to study law with Archibald Carter. After completing his studies, he went into business with Judge Richmond Pearson in the law firm of Meroney and Pearson. In 1828, Meroney built a home on Salisbury Street. During the 1830s, Meroney shared this home with schoolteacher Peter Stuart Ney.

GRAVE OF PETER STEWART NEY. Ney lies buried at Third Creek Presbyterian Church in Rowan County. His tombstone reads, "In memory of Peter Stewart Ney a native of France and soldier of the French Revolution under Napoleon Bonaparte who departed this life November 15, 1846, aged 77 years." (Courtesy of Davidson College Archives.)

COMMENCEMENT DAY. A wagon carrying students in the annual commencement parade passes the Bank of Davie on the way to the picnic grounds. On commencement day, the parade began at the Cherry Street school building, went down Main Street, circled the old courthouse, and returned up Main Street to the arbor at the Masonic picnic grounds for the commencement program. (Courtesy of Carol and Lisa LeGrand.)

DAVIE COUNTY SCHOOL COMMENCEMENT PARADE. The annual school parade goes down Main Street through town. The Bank of Davie appears in the background, and the hotel can be seen in the left of the picture.

GRADED SCHOOL. Mocksville, N. C.

MOCKSVILLE GRADED SCHOOL. Located on Cherry Street, the school was built in 1910 and paid for by town bonds. With classes for grades first through fifth, the six-room school opened in the fall of 1911. Prof. Henry Pardue served as the first principal. The faculty consisted of Pattie Battle and Linda Clement. The building was remodeled in 1976 for administrative offices of the Davie County School System.

FIRST GRADE, 1920. Students at the Mocksville Graded School include, from left to right, (first row) Jane McGuire, John Rich, Polly Grant Wilson, Mary Luna Smith, Jeffy Benson, Clinton Ward, Alice Carr, Helen Charles Carter, Mary Wilson Stone Rodwell, Ruth Angell, and Ella Mae Nail; (second row) Hazel Walker, Mildred Thompson, unidentified, Katherine Frost Bunch, Wilma Graves, Sadie Hall Woodruff, ? Hutchens, Sarah Dwiggins, and Katherine Crawford; (third row) Everette Blackwood, Woodrow Neely, unidentified, Clarence Wall, Robert Miller, Henry Poplin, Carroll Howard, unidentified, and Walter Leach.

73

MOCKSVILLE HIGH SCHOOL. The school opened in 1924 with grades 6–12. After Davie High School opened in 1956, the building functioned as an elementary school and was torn down in 1972. The Brock Building now stands in its place. (Courtesy of Lash and Cyrette Sanford.)

MOCKSVILLE HIGH SCHOOL GYM. Mocksville High School's first gymnasium, constructed during the 1920s, consisted of a wooden building heated by four pot bellied stoves in each corner. The original gym was replaced in the 1950s, with rollaway bleachers that could seat up to 1,100 people. It also had two practice courts. Dressing rooms and shower facilities for both home and visiting teams existed. (Courtesy of Hugh S. Larew.)

MOCKSVILLE HIGH SCHOOL FOOTBALL TEAM, 1936. Pictured are Joseph Ferebee, quarterback; Thomas Ferebee, fullback Holland Chaffin, left halfback; George Tutterow, right halfback; William Merrill, right end; Warren Ferebee, right tackle; Robert Evans, right guard; C. F. Leach, center; Robert Hendricks, left guard; Rufus Angell, left tackle; and Gordon Tomlinson, left end. Team members not pictured include Kim Sheek, Joe F. Stroud, and Clay Tutterow. (Courtesy of Ray Tutterow.)

MOCKSVILLE HIGH SCHOOL EIGHTH GRADE, 1927. Students pictured are, from left to right, (first row) Philip Kirk, John Rich, Billie Thompson, Katherine Frost, Sara Dwiggins, and Addie Mae Caudell; (second row) Ella Mae Nail, Louise Chaffin, Ruby Bowls, Annie Mae Grubbs, Thelma Poplin, Grace Bowls, and Velma Foster; (third row) Woodrow Neely, Roy Collette, Everette Seamon, Fred Carter, Helen Jones, Mozel Cope, Helen Charles, and Henry Poplin; (fourth row) John Lanier, Hubert Carter, Frank Stonestreet, Ruth Allen, Pauline Sisk, Margaret James, and Jane McGuire; (fifth row) Paul Hendricks, Champ Clark, Millard Anderson, Henry Tutterow, Everett Horn, Polly Tutterow, and Beatrice Seamon.

MOCKSVILLE HIGH SCHOOL FUTURE CLASS OF 1930. Known class members in the photograph, made in 1928, include, from left to right, (first row) unidentified, Blanche Leach, Eleanor Cain, unidentified, Lucille Allen, Brewster Grant, and Ruth Foster; (second row) Jane Woodruff (second from left with glasses) and Vada Merrill (fourth from left); (third row) Jane Bradley (left end) and Mable Barnhardt (fourth from left); (fourth row) Hanes Clement (fourth from left) and Mary McGuire (fifth from left); (fifth row) Frank Sain (with glasses) and Raleigh Baker (to the right of Sain); (sixth row) A. Benson (left).

MOCKSVILLE HIGH SCHOOL, 1931. Students pictured are, from left to right, (first row) Laura Ritchie, Annie Lois Ferebee, Katherine Frost, Sara Dwiggins, Nannie Barneycastle, Ella Mae Nail, and Shirley Lowery; (second row) Ella Mae Campbell, Bessie Chaffin, Annie Mae Grubbs, Ruth Ferebee, Sadie Mae Foster, Edna Beaver, and Geneva Angell; (third row) Louise Davis, Helen Jones, Jane McGuire, Mildred "Billie" Thompson, Frances Smith, Helen Brewer, and Francis Loftin; (fourth row) Philip Kirk, Fred Carter, John Rich, Joe Whitley, Henry Poplin, and Millard "Buster" Foster; (fifth row) Roy Collette, Frank Stonestreet, Woodrow Wilson, and Paul Hendricks.

MOCKSVILLE HIGH SCHOOL, CLASS OF 1942. The students are, from left to right, (first row) Hallie Foster, Ruth Foster, and Worth Hendricks; (second row) Helen Page, Johnsie Bracken, Vernice Vick, Lucille Gaither, Maggie Foster, Mary Dwiggins, Evelyn Turner, Bertie Mae Kimmer, Jane Sheek, and Frances Ramsey; (third row) Dorothy Clement, Sheek Bowden, Geraldine McCullough, Laura Lee Carter, Ruth Smith, Faye Dwiggins, Laura Bowles, Frankie Whitaker, and Amanda Ferebee; (fourth row) Geraldine Stonestreet, Helen Howard, Marie Johnson, Jessie Maynard, Edna Lanier, Tilthia Raye McCullough, Eloise McCorkle, Hazel Charles, and Eva Mae Smith; (fifth row) Pansy Evans, Irvin Hepler, Vada Boger, Henry S. Anderson, Phillip Stonestreet, William Summers, Craig Boger, and W. D. Booie Jr; (sixth row) Clarence Gobble, Gilbert Sofley, Jessie Stroud, Wylene Bailey, Mabel Woodward, Frankie Call, Elmer Hendrix, and Harold Cope Young; (seventh row) Charlie Angell, Henry Short, John Henry Pope, Hugh Larew, Johnny Haire, Holland Holton, and William Fink. (Courtesy of Hugh S. Larew.)

MOCKSVILLE HIGH SCHOOL GIRLS BASKETBALL TEAM, 1937. Team members include Ruth Dunn, Martha Lee Craven, Eleanor Woodruff, Louise Miller, Ozelle Miller, Myrtle Marrs, and the coach, C. R. Crenshaw.

LAST SENIOR CLASS OF MOCKSVILLE HIGH SCHOOL. The senior class of 1956 includes, from left to right, mascots Barbara Tutterow and Donnie Lakey; (first row) Hazel Clement, Nancy Bates, June Greene, Harriet Tutterow, Faye Wilson, Jeanette Butner, Patricia Smith, Jo Ann Gaither Ratledge, Carolyn Reavis, Kathleen Gaither, Lois Whitaker, and Geraldine White; (second row) Molly Waters, Doris McDaniel Gaither, Joan Smith, Julia Allen, Yvonne Hutchins, Ermon Beauchamp, Colean Blackwelder, Christine Beauchamp, Anne Richardson, Bonnie Shaw Troutman, Janice Smith, and Ona Robertson; (third row) Rebecca Carter, Linda Owings, Gail Walker, Mary Alice Boger, Betty Jo Foster, Lynda Crawford, Helen Laird, Shelby Richardson, Marcia Lagle, Betty Edwards, Patty Taylor, and Louise Keaton; (fourth row) Robert Mabe, Bailey Walker, Grady White, Homer Reeves, Bob Kiger, Billy O'Neal, Alton Sheek, Everette Glasscock, Kenneth Howell, Floyd Greene, and Tennyson Anderson; (fifth row) Henry Shutt, Johnny Etchison, Morgan Chaffin, Jimmy Kelly, Melver Culler, Gaither Sanford, and Billy Sell.

MOCKSVILLE HIGH SCHOOL BASKETBALL TEAM, 1940. Known members of the team include Nell Livengood, Marie Johnson, Jane Sheek, Laura Smith, Katharine Ferebee, Inez Williams, and Geraldine Stonestreet.

VARSITY TEAM, 1957. The women's basketball team for Davie County Consolidated High School featured, from left to right, (first row) Carolyn Boger, Norma Jean Cornatzer, Joan Shore, Lucy King, Alice Anderson, Peggy Lamb, and Camilla Jarvis; (second row) Nancy Cozart, Alma White, Sue Howard, Floretta Collette, Edith Smith, Linda Garwood, and coach Jack Ward.

MAJORETTES. The photograph shows Davie County Consolidated High School majorettes Sue Brewer (left) and Judy Scott in 1960.

DAVIE HOMECOMING QUEEN OF 1958. Principal Dave Stillwell crowns the homecoming queen, Faye Dean Williams, daughter of F. E. and Alma Jones Williams of Advance. Each member of the football team selected a girl to sponsor for homecoming queen. The entire student body of Davie High School voted on the selected girls. The football team selected the final queen from the five finalists determined by the student body vote. Halftime ceremonies at the Friday night football game included presentation of all contestants.

MOCKSVILLE HOMECOMING QUEEN. Carol Miller, daughter of Sheek and Louise Hendricks Miller, received her crown as homecoming queen at an October football game in 1955 while escorted by Billy Sell, son of W. J. B. and Roberta Jane Koontz Sell.

Four

FACES AND FAMILIES

MARY JANE HEITMAN
(1886–1962). In addition to
teaching English at Salem
Academy in Winston-Salem,
Mary Jane Heitman worked on
the staff of the *Davie County
Enterprise* as the society
editor. She authored a column
called The Corner Cupboard,
in which she wrote about
the history of the county.
Heitman served as Davie
County historian for many
years. She also taught Sunday
school at First Methodist
Church of Mocksville for
almost 50 years. A former
student paid her tribute saying,
"Surely, I am voicing the
sentiments of any number of
Salem Academy girls of those
days, when I declare that
study led by Miss Heitman
was a happy, rewarding
experience." (Courtesy of
Lash and Cyrette Sanford.)

JUNIOR ORDER HOME LODGE, C. 1907. Members pose in front of their meeting place at the old Bethel Schoolhouse. The Mocksville Council No. 226 of the Junior Order United American Mechanics came into existence on July 24, 1907. The fraternal organization provided an insurance reserve for its members and American flags to fly above public school buildings.

CENTENNIAL CELEBRATION. Mocksville Masonic Lodge members at their centennial celebration in 1950 include, from left to right, (first row, kneeling) Luke M. Graves, Rufus Sanford Jr., James R. York, Joe Patner, Raymond Siler, unidentified, John P. LeGrand, J. C. Jones, and J. C. Dwiggins; (second row) C. F. Leach, S. Anderson, unidentified, Dr. Wilkins, John S. Haire, Percy Brown, Dr. Henry C. Sprinkle, George Thompson, Leslie Daniel, Jim Thompson, Ed Avett, and Gray Hendricks; (third row) Marvin Waters, Jim Thompson, J. G. Crawford, Kirk Arnold, R.B. Sanford, Cecil Little, Glenn Hammer, Red Hartman, Atlas Smoot, D. Roscoe Stroud, and Knox Johnstone; (fourth row) Duke Tutterow, unidentified, Sam Latham, Joe Ferebee, Roy Holthouser, Nick Mando, unidentified, Dave Rankin, unidentified, E. Cecil Morris, Sam Short, unidentified, John Waters, Col. Jacob Stewart, Sam Short, Henry Short, Charles Farthing, unidentified, Bill Merrill, Graham Madison, Eugene Smith, unidentified, and Grant Daniel. (Courtesy of Taylor Slye.)

ROTARY CLUB OF MOCKSVILLE. Twenty-nine original members chartered the Rotary Club in 1945 with the purpose of working together to lend strength and a unified approach to community advancement. J. K. Sheek served as the first president of the club and T. J. Caudell as secretary. The Rotary Hut opened in December 1946 at the corner of Salisbury and Sanford Streets. The building cost about $4,000 and was financed through the sale of stock to club members. The Hut was burned down to make way for parking in June 2007. The old Parnell House can be seen through the trees at the right of the Hut.

MOCKSVILLE WOMAN'S CLUB. Members of the Mocksville Woman's Club dust the banisters on the circular staircase at Cooleemee Plantation in preparation for their annual tour of homes. The cost of the tour in 1962 was $1, which included access to eight homes. (Courtesy of Peter W. Hairston.)

DAVIE GRAYS. The Davie Grays Chapter of the United Daughters of the Confederacy organized in 1930 with 20 members. The chapter named itself after the Davie County Confederate Regiment commanded by Jesse A. Clement. In 1933, the UDC held its fourth district meeting in Mocksville. The ladies of Davie Grays, under the leadership of their president, Mary Heitman, opened the doors of the Masonic Hall and entertained more than 100 UDC daughters from across North Carolina. Throughout its history, the members of this chapter supported many local charities in Mocksville. After 60 years, the chapter disbanded in 1990. It ranked as one of the oldest chapters in North Carolina.

DR. LESTER POINDEXTER MARTIN (1898–1963). The photograph shows Lester Martin at 12 years of age. Born in Davie County on January 1, 1898, to Dr. W. C. and Frances Eaton Martin, Martin graduated from Mocksville High School in 1914, received a Bachelor of Science degree from Wake Forest University in 1918, and his degree in medicine from Jefferson Medical College in 1920. Martin began practicing medicine with his father in Mocksville in 1923. He served as Davie County quarantine officer from 1925 to 1939, county coroner from 1938 to 1942, and was a member on the County Welfare Board from 1923 to 1936. (Courtesy of Lester P. Martin Jr.)

MARTIN ROWAN CHAFFIN, SEPTEMBER 26, 1917. M. R. Chaffin (1828–1925) served as county surveyor and U.S. commissioner for a number of years. Born in 1828, he ranked as one of Mocksville's oldest citizens. He walked to town from his home on Depot Street once or twice a day. Chaffin lived during the administrations of 23 presidents and cultivated corn in Mocksville near the public square when Martin Van Buren served as president.

WILLIAM ALEXANDER MERONEY (1826–1909). William A. Meroney served as sheriff of Davie County from 1860 to 1866. He married Anna Hanes of Forsyth County and moved there in the late 1860s. He poses here with his grandson, William D. Meroney.

CALVIN COWLES SANFORD FAMILY. This family photograph, made about 1909, includes, from left to right, (front row) Mary Louise Sanford, Calvin Cowles Sanford, Mary Brown Sanford, and William Lafayette Sanford; (second row) John Calvin Sanford, Hugh Adams Sanford, Laura Sanford, Bob Faucette, Edwin Cowles Sanford, unidentified, Rufus Brown Sanford, and Thomas Franklin Sanford. (Courtesy of Lash and Cyrette Sanford.)

IN THE BACKYARD. The C. C. Sanford family relaxes in their backyard in 1907. Pictured from left to right are Laura Sanford Faucette, unidentified (reclining), Mary Sanford, Mary Katherine Faucette (baby), C. C. Sanford, Robert T. Faucette, and Mary Brown Sanford. (Courtesy of Hugh S. Larew.)

EPHRAIM LASH GAITHER (1850–1943).
Gaither studied law under Chief Justice
Richmond Pearson at Richmond Hill Law
School. Admitted to the bar in 1875, he
practiced in Mocksville for approximately
60 years. He served as solicitor of the Davie
County Inferior Court during the first
years of his practice. During World War I,
he chaired the County Board of Defense.
Gaither served as vice president of the
North Carolina Bar Association and was a
member of the American Bar Association.
He served as a director of the Wachovia
Bank and Trust Company and president
of the Bank of Davie from 1916 to 1934.
(Courtesy of Lash and Cyrette Sanford.)

E. L. GAITHER FAMILY. Pictured are Ephraim Lash Gaither and his wife, Florence Clement Gaither, with daughters Jane Hayden Gaither (seated), Adelaide Marshall Gaither (standing behind Jane), Dorothy S. Gaither (baby), and Sarah Hall Gaither. (Courtesy of Lash and Cyrette Sanford.)

LOUISE STROUD (1913–2008).
Daughter of the *Davie Record* editor, Stroud spent the first 12 years of her life living above the newspaper office. She received her Bachelor's degree in music from Salem College. Stroud served as the pianist and organist at the First Baptist Church for 61 years and taught piano lessons for 57 years. Stroud won numerous awards for her musical contributions. She loved to write and published a book, *Music Antic Notes*, about her recollections as a piano teacher. Stroud had many of her hymns, poems, and articles published. She wrote several episodes of *The Life of Miss Lizzie*, which was about a backwoods character with no formal education, and performed them at various community events. Stroud is perhaps best remembered for her newspaper column of recollections of Mocksville. In honor of "Miss Louise," more than 110 people, including many former students, donated to the purchase of a grand piano for the Brock Center, which was dedicated at a gala in January 2008.

JOHN AVERY FOSTER (1895–1986). Foster, known affectionately as "Mr. Avery," was a member of the Mocksville Police Department for 41 years. He became the first black deputy sheriff in North Carolina in 1954 and Mocksville town constable in 1965.

CHARLES "RED" SELLS (1894–1942).
Cicero W. Sell, living in Cooleemee,
lured by the smell of grease paint
and the roar of the crowds, ran away
and joined the Sparks Circus. He
became the world famous clown
Charles W. "Red" Sells. Sells later
worked for the Ringling Brothers
Circus, Sells-Floto Circus, and the
Hagenbeck-Wallace Circus. His act
included a trained dog, pigs, and a
goose that pulled his goose mobile.
(Both, courtesy of the *Salisbury Post*.)

THOMAS EDWARD "BUNN" SEATS (1910–1992). Seats, a native of Farmington, pitched in the major leagues for both the Detroit Tigers (1940) and the Brooklyn Dodgers (1945). He made his major league debut in 1940 against the Philadelphia Athletics at Shibe Park. His career 57 game included two shutouts. (Courtesy of Charles "Muggs" Smith.)

CENTER BARBECUE. Pictured from left to right, Duke Tutterow, Clay Boger, Clay Tutterow, and Clyde Dyson prepare pork shoulders for a Center Community barbecue during the 1960s. About 5,000 pounds of pork are cooked at each annual barbecue to raise funds for the Center Volunteer Fire Department and the Center Community Development Association. (Courtesy of Ray Tutterow.)

L. M. TUTTEROW STORE.
Luther Martin "Luke" Tutterow
and his wife, Nancy Ellen
Tutterow, stand on the porch of
their store, which was located
across from the Center Arbor.
Tutterow owned a generator
and supplied power to the
Center Arbor and the Center
United Methodist Church
until electricity reached
the area. The Tutterows
also ran the local telephone
exchange from their home.
(Courtesy of Ray Tutterow.)

LUKE TUTTEROW'S LITTLE CLOTHES. In
1935, a mystery person gave Tutterow a
miniature pair of pants at a community
Christmas party. The following year,
he received a matching coat and suit
of underwear. In 1937, he received a
vest and tiny socks. Rebecca Talbert
of Advance later admitted sending
the articles of clothing, knowing
that Tutterow loved a good practical
joke. Tutterow served as a Davie
County commissioner from 1932 to
1940. (Courtesy of Ray Tutterow.)

CENTER UNITED METHODIST CHURCH CHOIR. The photograph, taken around 1937, includes, from left to right, (first row) Mary Everhart Seaford, Clara Vanzant Tutterow, Theo Ijames Tutterow, Alice Evans Dyson, Annie Walker, Johnsie Boger Spears, Vera Vanzant Dwiggins, Jimmy Neal Anderson (baby), Sarah Anderson, Vauda Merrell Minor, Ethel Anderson, Mazie Vanzant Merrell, and Iva Anderson Koch; (second row) Robert Duke Tutterow, Charles Tomlinson, Ollie Odus Tutterow, J.C. Anderson, James Millard Anderson, James Garfield Anderson, Luke M. Tutterow, William Floyd Tutterow, Henry Wilson "Bo" Tutterow, and Loa Dwiggins. (Courtesy of Ray Tutterow.)

FOUR VAGABONDS. A few Mocksville residents witnessed the brief stop of several visitors to town on August 29, 1918. Henry Ford, Thomas Edison, and Harvey Firestone pulled into the square and asked for a drink of water, which residents obtained from the well. The men passed through Mocksville and Winston-Salem on their way to Virginia. Upon arrival in Winston-Salem, city fathers hosted a luncheon for the visitors at the Forsyth Country Club, shown here. Pictured are, from left to right, James G. Hanes, Henry Dwire, B. S. Womble, Harvey Firestone Sr., A. H. Eller, Thomas Edison, Frank Dunklee, John Gilmer, Henry Ford, B. F. Huntley, unidentified, P. H. Hanes, Ray Johnson, Powell Gilmer, Harvey Firestone Jr., Will Watkins, Norman Stockton, and unidentified. The fourth vagabond, naturalist John Burroughs, departed by train from Asheville the day before this visit. For several years around 1920, the four men participated in lengthy motor camping excursions, earning their nickname of "the four vagabonds." (Courtesy of Forsyth County Public Library Photograph Collection.)

UNCLE JOHN MARTIN (1849–1951). Martin is shown here with his old horn made from snuff cans. The horn used to call worshippers to camp meeting services held on the Smith Grove Methodist Church grounds. (Courtesy of Gwyn and Ann Smith.)

SMITH GROVE METHODIST CHURCH. Members pose in front of the church during homecoming in 1935. Smith Grove Church grew out of the camp meetings held at the old Whitaker Church, built on the east side of Dutchman's Creek in 1780. The wood frame church was built in 1877. (Courtesy of Gene Plott.)

TAKING A BREAK. George Allen (left), Charlie Frye (center), and Wesley Allen rest during their work at Duke Smith's home on Rainbow Road. (Courtesy of Estelle Smith.)

GAITHER SAWMILL, 1912. William Guy Gaither Sr. (front left), Ralph Gaither (front center), Thomas A. Gaither (front, sitting in wagon), and David Richardson (back, sitting in wagon) pose at Thomas A. Gaither's sawmill in the Sheffield area around 1912. The other four men are unidentified. The dog is unidentified but of good stock. (Courtesy of Marie Roth.)

TEA PARTY, 1902. A tea party held in 1902 at the home of Louiza Furches Etchison raised funds to purchase a bell for Eaton's Baptist Church. Family members and guests include, from left to right, (first row) John Wesley Etchison, Nana Cain Etchison, Orrell Etchison (baby), Louise Furches Etchison, Susan Etchison Eaton, Maida Eaton, Mossa Eaton, Joseph Wesley Eaton, and Annie Eaton; (second row) Mattie Boger, unidentified, Allie Clifford, Mattie McClamrock, Mary Hunter, Gaston L. White, Martha Stonestreet, Millie Hutchins, Sebia Stonestreet Hutchins, John Ray Eaton, Flora Harding, Louise Eaton, Lewis Alexander Etchison, Mrs. Oscar Hutchins, and Oscar Hutchins; (third row) Richard Eaton, Sam Stonestreet, William Hutchins, John Naylor, Susie Hutchins Naylor, Susan Eaton Naylor, Elizabeth Naylor, ? Penry, unidentified, Braxton Stonestreet, Flora Hunter, ? Penry, Ina Naylor, and Sallie McClamrock; (roof) John Andy Naylor, Hands Hunter, Euly Grubbs, Boyce Cain, Boone Stonestreet, and Martin Eaton. (Courtesy of Betty Etchison West.)

CAIN FAMILY, 1898. The family of James Harrison and Elizabeth Amy Frost Cain includes, from left to right, (first row) Elizabeth Amy Frost Cain; Margaret Cain, who married G. M. Kirkman; and James Harrison Cain, a veteran of the Confederate Navy; (second row) John Boyce Cain, who married Ina Naylor; and Effie Eleanor Cain; (third row) Dr. J. W. Rodwell holding his child; Quilla Cain Rodwell; Harrison James Cain; John Wesley Etchison; and his wife, Mary Nana Cain Etchison. (Courtesy of Betty Etchison West.)

EATON FAMILY. Eaton family members are, from left to right, (first row) Columbus Eaton, Jim Ferebee, Elizabeth Ferebee Eaton, Alex Eaton, and Frank Eaton; (second row) Betty Eaton, Susan Eaton, Philivia Eaton, Richard Eaton, and Tom Eaton. (Courtesy of Bill Ferebee.)

LEWIS ALEXANDER ETCHISON (1865–1940). Everyone in the Cana community referred to Etchinson as "Uncle Lukey." A well-known beekeeper, Etchison always said, "The bees have taught me much concerning life, so in return I'll be glad to share it with you." He used his skills as an inventor and cabinetmaker to fashion his bee hives. He also invented a cotton picker, tobacco setter, grain cleaner, and a honey extractor. The photograph shows Etchison with his secretary made by Lamb Taylor, a Farmington furniture maker. The secretary now stands in the history room at the Davie County Public Library.

ANNIE LAURIE ETCHISON (1908–1988). As a Special Forces librarian, Etchison served at Langley Field, Virginia; Alaska; the Philippines; Japan; Korea; and Europe from 1941 to 1977. Etchison also authored several articles, including *Library Music Hour, Books for the Soldier,* and *Soldiers Read at Langley Field.* (Courtesy of Betty Etchison West.)

JAMES WALTER ETCHISON (1912–2010). Etchison worked for Pan American Airlines for 36 years. In 1939, he served as flight engineer on the *Yankee Clipper,* the first commercial flight across the Atlantic Ocean from Baltimore to Marseille, France. In 1958, he served as flight engineer on the first jet commercial flight across the Atlantic from New York to Paris. While working at Pan American, he also performed test flights with Charles Lindbergh. (Courtesy of Betty Etchison West.)

HENDRICKS FAMILY. This home, built by John Hendricks in 1833, stands on Dutchman's Creek. From left to right are "Babe" Boles, Louiza Foote, Monroe Hendricks, Mattie Lou Davis, Bynum Davis, Martha Ann Redmond Hendricks, Dwight Davis (seated boy), Elmo Davis, Robert Davis, and Cora Hendricks Davis.

WARD FAMILY. The family poses in front of their Pino area home, which no longer exists. Family members include, from left to right, (front row) Claudius Ward, Brian Ward, Louise Miller Ward, and Laura Ward; (second row) Eloise Ward, Lola Ward Carter, Marvin Stacey Ward, Flare Ferebee, and Zella Ward Ferebee. (Courtesy of Bill Ferebee.)

DAVID RICHARDSON FAMILY, 1912. The family consists of Elsie Richardson (left), Elma Richardson (child with doll), Carrie Beck (back), Mary Louise "Molly" Beck Richardson (sitting), Mae Richardson (child on lap), and David Lafayette Richardson with his two mules, Barney and George. The family lived near the fork of Turkey Foot Road and Log Cabin Road in Sheffield. (Courtesy of Marie Roth.)

CRAVEN FAMILY. The Craven family held a reunion at their homestead on Sain Road in 1939. (Courtesy of C. C. Craven.)

ALICE SMOOT (1863–1904). Alice was born into slavery and owned by the Blaylock family. The family sold her mother before emancipation. After the Civil War, Alice married James W. Smoot. The couple had one daughter, Martha Smoot. Alice worked for the Collette family. (Courtesy of Frances Collette Dunn.)

TURTLE SOUP. R. S. Smith caught the 36-pound turtle from a lake on Fred Bahnson's Win Mock Farm. Bahnson remembered that sheriff Ernie Shore of Forsyth County mentioned that he would like to have a nice freshwater turtle. Shown on the courthouse steps are, from left to right, Sheriff Shore, the turtle, and Fred Bahnson. (Courtesy of Bert Bahnson.

Five

OUTSKIRTS OF TOWN

HALL'S FERRY. C. A. Hall Sr. received a charter in 1875 preventing the establishment of another ferry within three miles of his ferry crossing, which was located at the site of present day Highway 158 at the Katherine Crosby Bridge. The nearest ferry downstream was Idol's (formerly Douthit's) Ferry. The closest ferry upstream was Griffith's (later Styer's) Ferry. The Halls charged 40¢ for a round trip with a two-horse wagon. Passengers on foot crossed for 5¢; however, preachers crossed for free. Horseless carriages, or automobiles, paid $1 to cross. In 1913, the commissioners in Forsyth and Davie Counties decided to build a bridge at the crossing. For a year, the ferryboat crossed in the shadow of the growing steel structure and ceased operating after the opening of the bridge. (Courtesy of the Clemmons branch of the Forsyth County Public Library system.)

SOUTH RIVER BRIDGE. The bridge replaced the ferry on the South River at Highway 601 on the line between Davie and Rowan Counties. Lindsay Foard Grist Mill can be seen at right in the photograph. Three members of the bridge committee, P. B. Beard, P. A. Hartman, and C. G. Bailey, stand on the bridge. (Courtesy of the Rowan Museum.)

HUNTING CREEK BRIDGE. Horse and buggies cross the old bridge located at today's Highway 64 West and Hunting Creek. The man on the bridge has been identified as Z. N. Anderson. (Courtesy of Taylor Slye.)

ADVANCE ROLLER MILL, 1914. The mill operated from the late 1880s to the mid-1930s. It stood on the north end of Advance, across the road from the railroad depot. W. A. Bailey and B. R. Bailey owned the mill. John Wiley Sheek worked as the miller. Martin Miller, Bob Williams, and Charlie Ward worked in the mill. The mill ground wheat and corn for local residents. It also packaged and sold its own flour and cornmeal. (Courtesy of Edith Shutt Zimmerman.)

ADVANCE COTTON GIN, 1913. W. A. Bailey owned the gin that was located in lower Advance. The photograph shows Hazel and Harry Sheek with their horse Mag. Note the bales of cotton stacked on the side porch of the gin. (Courtesy of Edith Shutt Zimmerman.)

ADVANCE DEPOT, AROUND 1900. The first train stopped in Davie County at the Advance Depot on May 8, 1891. Many members of the community came on horseback and in horse and buggy to see the big "Iron Horse." The depot also provided a social gathering place for the community on Sunday afternoons. Four passenger trains and two freight trains ran every day. Gus Allison served as the first depot agent. The railroad closed the depot, and the building was torn down in 1953. (Courtesy of Edith Shutt Zimmerman.)

W. C. WHITE AND COMPANY STORE. This store, owned by William Colfax White, sold general merchandise in the Advance community. In front of the old store are, from left to right, Albert Holder, Will Shermer, an unidentified salesman, and Bonce Bailey. The store burned in 1917. White owned four stores and served as postmaster in Advance. (Courtesy of Robert Stafford.)

ADVANCE ACADEMY COMMENCEMENT, 1910. The students wearing ribbons were ushers; those wearing scarves were marshals. The Smith boys were sons of L. L. Smith, pastor of the Methodist Church. The students include, from left to right, (first row) Luna Vogler Hartman, Annie Faircloth Hall, teacher Mary Henry Thompson, Laura Shutt, Mame Markland Wyatt, Clara Orrell Hartman, Edna Cornatzer McAbee, Emma Markland Mason, and Robert Cornatzer; (second row) Eugene Smith, George Smith, unidentified, Frank Smithdeal, Georgia Lippard Hartley, G. Alex Tucker, Clara Peebles, Josephine Hartman Vogler, Myrtle March Carter, Agnes Peebles, Grace Faircloth, Lucille Peebles Greene, and Charlie Shutt; (third row) Rufus Markland, Tommy Phelps, George Mock, Augustus Vogler Cornatzer, Cora Hartman, Lizzie Vogler Hartman, Bailey Tucker, Glen Smithdeal, unidentified commencement speaker (white hair), Glenn Bailey, and Lelia Orrell Ziglar; (fourth row) Bryant Bailey, Deems Ward Mock, Willie Shutt, Ethel Smithdeal, Eva Leonard Tate, Beatrice Thompson Ripple, Bennie Orrell, and Walter Shutt. (Courtesy of Edith Shutt Zimmerman.)

WILL HENDRIX STORE. The Will Hendrix Store was located in downtown Advance, and community members often gathered here to tell "tall tales." From left to right, Lindsay Watkins, Dr. Thomas T. Watkins, John Etchison, Will Hendrix, Ance Cornatzer, Lindsay Cornatzer, and Sam Bailey pose in this photograph. (Courtesy of Edith Shutt Zimmerman.)

COOLEEMEE COTTON MILL. Charles Fisher built the first mill at the shoals in the 1830s. The land was deeded to Cooleemee Water, Power, and Manufacturing Company on July 22, 1899. The new cotton mill, constructed around 1900, ran at full production in 1903. This ranks as one of the earliest known photographs of the mill. A windmill can be seen on the left in the picture.

ERWIN COTTON MILL. Built on the banks of the South Yadkin River, the cotton mill in Cooleemee operated under various names over the years: Shoals Cotton Mill; Cooleemee Water, Power, and Manufacturing Company; Cooleemee Cotton Mill; and in 1906, Erwin Cotton Mill No. 3. The mill, owned by Burlington Industries, closed in 1969.

COOLEEMEE DAM. The dam stood at the shoals of the South Yadkin River. Built of rock quarried at the site, the 477-foot long and 10-foot high dam was completed in November 1900.

MILLRACE. A 1.5-mile long canal, this millrace began at the dam and ran along the river down to the mill. It measured 100 feet wide and 20 feet deep. Water from the canal poured through a large grill into two giant water turbines, supplying power to the entire community.

COOLEEMEE COTTON MILL DRIVE WHEEL. Belts and pulleys, driven from a central power source, operated all machines that carded the fiber and spun the yarn and looms that wove the cloth. Pictured here is a power-generating drive wheel that is connected by ropes to a similar wheel above. Turned by a shaft, this wheel connected to water turbines that were fed by the millrace. This photograph, taken under the mill during installation by the Ladshaw and Ladshaw Company of Greenville, South Carolina, dates to 1899.

MILL VILLAGE. The mill company built and maintained about 360 houses for mill workers who lived in Cooleemee. Constructed of heart of pine, many houses still stand today. The small homes, painted white, green, and "punkin" yellow, featured three or four rooms, a front porch, and back stoops. Electricity and running water arrived in the 1930s. Mill management sold the houses to those employees who wanted to buy in 1954.

COMPANY STORE. The J. N. Ledford Sore opened on the square in 1901, just after the mill opened.

COOLEEMEE GRADED SCHOOL. With the foundation laid in 1901, the county's first graded school, facing Watts Street and directly across from a Presbyterian church, opened in December 1902. The building featured two stories, 10 rooms, and an assembly hall that also served as a chapel. The old school became a primary school after the new brick high school opened. The Presbyterian church can be seen in the background, behind the old school. The picture postcard was mailed in 1918 to Houston Tutterow at Camp Joseph E. Johnston, a World War I training camp located in Florida. (Courtesy of Ray Tutterow.)

COOLEEMEE PLANTATION. The Hairston homestead, completed in 1855, appears on the National Register of Historic Places and has been designated as a National Historic Landmark. The Anglo-Grecian villa represented a complete departure in design and detail from any prior architecture in Piedmont, North Carolina. Designed by New York architect W. H. Ranlett, the house cost $10,438 to build. The outbuildings on the plantation consisted of a smokehouse, kitchen, dairy, icehouse, carriage house, office, stables, milk barn, chicken house, granary, corncrib, and kennel. (Courtesy of Peter W. Hairston.)

JUDGE PETER WILSON HAIRSTON (1913–2007). Born at Cooleemee Plantation, Hairston graduated from the University of North Carolina Law School in 1935. In 1954, he established a law practice in Mocksville and maintained it until 1977. At that time, Hairston became the second resident in the history of the county to be appointed as a Superior Court judge. Hairston also served three terms in the North Carolina House of Representatives. In the photograph, Judge Hairston sits in the main hall of Cooleemee Plantation. (Courtesy of Peter W. Hairston.)

FERRY AT COOLEEMEE PLANTATION. The Hairston family's private ferry operated across the Yadkin River from Davie County to Davidson County. In an interview, Judge Hairston told the following story of Righteous, the ferryman: "Righteous . . . had the very privileged job of ferryman. It was privileged because most of the time, he lay on the bank of the river. The system was my father would go to the foot of the top terrace and call for Righteous, so that the ferry would be there waiting for him when he drove down to the river. One day he called and called, and Righteous didn't answer. Righteous was under the tree on the other side of the river asleep. My father boomed, 'Righteous, if you don't get across here and get me right now, I'm going to come over there and throw you in the river.' Well, Righteous came and got him, but on the next day, crowds heard Righteous saying, 'Marse Peter say he gonna throw me in the river. Now, how he gonna do that when the ferry is on my side of the river?'" (Courtesy of Peter W. Hairston.)

EPISCOPAL CHURCH OF THE ASCENSION SUNDAY SCHOOL, C. 1910. The Episcopal Church of the Ascension in Fork was consecrated in 1909. Ruth Hairston, Agnes Hairston, and Fanny Caldwell Hairston were instrumental in organizing the Sunday school. Prior to construction of the building, services were held at Cooleemee Plantation and Fulton Methodist Episcopal Church, South. (Courtesy of Peter W. Hairston.)

MAIN STREET, Farmington, N. C.

FARMINGTON. The village of Farmington formed part of a larger area originally known as the Bryan Settlement, but after the Revolutionary War, many of the early settlers left the area and moved west. Following the migration of new settlers from Currituck County in the early 1800s, the community, then known as Little Currituck, began to flourish, and business began to thrive. The community adopted the name Farmington with the establishment of a post office in 1837. (Courtesy of Ron Williams.)

SANFORD & SMITH, General Merchandise, Farmington, N. C.

SANFORD AND SMITH. C. C. Sanford and a Mr. Smith operated the general store in Farmington from the early 1900s until around 1911, at which time G. H. Graham and C. A. Hartman acquired the business, operating as Graham and Company. The store carried dry goods, notions, shoes, groceries, and clothing. G. H. Graham managed the day-to-day operations. The store also served as a headquarters for community political meetings, as Hartman and Graham were staunch Republicans. (Courtesy of Ron Williams.)

FARMINGTON ROLLER MILL, Farmington, N. C.

FARMINGTON ROLLER MILL. The mill, known as Furches and Ellis in 1883, was A. W. Ellis and Company by 1890. According to an ad in the *Davie Record*, dated May 4, 1914, the mill had operated over 30 years. The business operated as a flour, corn, and feed mill, as well as a sawmill. Luck Jarvis was the miller. Albert Wilson Ellis eventually gave the mill to Thomas Redmon and T. Herbert Nicholson. A steam whistle sounded each day at 12:00 p.m. for lunch and then again at 1:00 p.m. for the return to work. The mill is thought to have burned around 1937. (Courtesy of Polly Lomax.)

FARMINGTON BAPTIST CHURCH. At a meeting held at the Union Academy building, the Farmington Baptist Church was constituted on December 29, 1878, with 39 members. On January 4, 1879, R. W. Crews, a church elder, was chosen as the first pastor. The church joined the South Yadkin Association in August 1879. The building committee selected a site for the church in 1881. In June 1882, the congregation dedicated its new building. (Courtesy of John Caudle.)

113

M. E. CHURCH, Farmington, N. C.

FARMINGTON METHODIST CHURCH. Olive Branch Methodist Church, organized in 1804, was the mother church for Farmington Methodist. On February 5, 1882, the last church service was held at Olive Branch and the congregation moved to the new church building in Farmington. The building was dedicated on the fifth Sunday in April 1882. The stained-glass windows were added in 1916, and other additions to the church followed in 1924 and 1950. W. C. Willson served as pastor from 1883 to 1886. (Courtesy of Ron Williams.)

M. E. PARSONAGE, Farmington, N. C.

FARMINGTON METHODIST CHURCH PARSONAGE. The parsonage was built around 1890, a few years after the nearby church building was completed. The house served as the Farmington Methodist Circuit parsonage until the early 1960s, when the congregation erected a new brick parsonage. (Courtesy of Ron Williams.)

CHARLES F. BAHNSON HOUSE. Bahnson, son of Bishop George Frederick Bahnson of Salem, was born in Lancaster, Pennsylvania, and came to Salem with his parents. He attended Salem Boys School and trained as a jeweler and optician. In 1865, he married Jane Amanda Johnson, the daughter of George Wesley Johnson of Farmington. Their home was built in the late 1870s. Bahnson practiced his profession in a small office near his home. (Both, courtesy of Ron Williams.)

FARMINGTON HIGH SCHOOL. The first high school in Davie County was held in 1907 in the old Farmington Academy Building. The building had been constructed around 1882 for about $1,500. The school was known as Farmington Academy until 1916, then Farmington High School. Until the new brick schoolhouse opened in 1919, classes were held in the wooden frame building. (Courtesy of Ron Williams.)

AUGUSTA SEMINARY. Prof. John D. Hodges opened the Augusta Seminary in 1888. In September 1897, it was sold at public auction to the North Carolina Yearly Meeting of Friends, who conducted a boarding school and held services in one room of the school building. After 1900, the Quakers discontinued the mission and the school. The abandoned building was then used for storage until it was struck by lightning on July 18, 1917. (Courtesy of John Fuller.)

HODGES BUSINESS COLLEGE.
The Hodges Business College operated in a brick building east of John D. Hodges's home. The college existed at the same time the Quaker School was held in the old Augusta Seminary building. Hodges operated the college from 1894 to the early 1900s, which was when he began to devote most of his time to his duties as superintendent of county schools. Hodges reopened the college and resumed teaching in 1909 and taught for a couple more years. After the school was discontinued, the first floor of the building was used for tenant housing until 1936. The building was then used for storage. Renovated in 2001, it now serves as a private home. (Courtesy of the *Salisbury Post.*)

J. D. HODGES HOUSE. The home, built in the 1880s, stands to the west of the 1894 Hodges Business College. It was the residence of John D. Hodges, a well-known and influential educator in Davie County. John D. and Sallie Augusta Hodges and three of their children can be seen on the porch. (Courtesy of John Fuller.)

BARNHARDT FAMILY HOME. The Jerusalem Township home, built in the 1870s or early 1880s, is one of the rare brick farmhouses built in Davie County. George Ephraim Barnhardt and wife Elizabeth Sarah Kindley Barnhardt lived there until their deaths. (Courtesy of the *Salisbury Post*.)

DAVIE COUNTY FARM. Records indicate that in antebellum Davie County, 90 percent of people in the county farmed for a living. The farms were self-sufficient. The families did their own work and grew or made most of what they ate, wore, and used. They raised only meager crops for sale and had very little money. (Courtesy of the *Salisbury Post*.)

HOBSON CARRIAGE. The Stokes's property and house remained in the Pearson family until the late 1840s, when Samuel Augustus Hobson purchased the property. The carriage shown in the picture, taken in the 1890s, predates the Civil War. (Courtesy of the *Salisbury Post.*)

JUDGE JOHN STOKES HOME. Stokes served as a captain in the Revolutionary War. He later became a member of the House of Commons and a member of the Constitutional Convention of 1789 that brought North Carolina into the Union. In 1790, Pres. George Washington appointed him as the first federal district judge for North Carolina. Stokes also practiced law in Salisbury. In 1788, he purchased a 275-acre tract of land next to Richmond Pearson. The same year, he married Pearson's daughter, Betsy, and as a wedding present, Pearson gave the couple 698 acres of land. In 1790, Stokes purchased four more acres and started construction on his home. Whether Stokes lived long enough to see his house finished is not known. He died in October 1790 on his way home from his only term on the bench in New Bern. Richmond Pearson served as administrator of his estate. (Courtesy of the *Salisbury Post.*)

FLAG RAISING CEREMONY, 1914. Holman's Crossroads School, a one-room schoolhouse, expanded by adding another classroom to the west side of the building. The flag raising ceremony celebrated completion of the classroom.

SPECIAL AIRMAIL DELIVERY. To mark the 20th anniversary of scheduled airmail service in the United States, President Roosevelt declared the week of May 15, 1938, National Airmail Week. On Thursday, May 19, 1938, over 1,700 one-day-only flights occurred to carry special airmail "covers" (envelopes). One such flight picked up and delivered airmail at the George Feezor Farm, located across from the Davie County High School site. Given the short landing field, the pilot had to come in at an angle to make the landing. Thirteen-year-old Hugh Larew rode his bicycle down to see the plane land and collected his first-day cover to add to his stamp collection. Postmaster John P. LeGrand reported that 80 letters traveled from Mocksville on this first-ever mail plane. (Courtesy of Hugh S. Larew.)

CANA STORE AND POST OFFICE. The structure, built around 1875 by James Harrison Cain, served Cana both as a general store and a post office. After Cain moved to Mocksville, John Boyce and Ina Naylor Cain operated the store. Ina Naylor Cain served as postmaster from 1919 to 1954, when the office closed. John Boyce Cain Jr. and Audrey Rands can be seen sweeping inside the old store (below). (Both, courtesy of Betty Etchison West.)

LAZY DAYS IN CANA.
Annie Laurie Etchison,
with Johnny (center)
and Billy Etchison
on her bicycle, stops
in front of the Cana
Store (below). (Both,
courtesy of Betty
Etchison West.)

VISITING WITH NEIGHBORS. The store in Cana provided a place to visit with neighbors. In the photograph below, John Walter Etchison appears with his friend Mary Cutler and two unidentified boys. (Both, courtesy of Betty Etchison West.)

CAIN HOUSE. Completed in 1926, Dodson Grubbs and John James built the house for John Boyce and Ina Naylor Cain. The Cains operated the Cana Store from 1934 to the mid-1960s. (Courtesy of Betty Etchison West.)

MARTHA SMOOT (1874–1939). Martha Smoot, wife of Will Smoot, lived near the Cana schoolhouse and worked for both the Cain and Etchison families. She stands in the photograph with her grandson Edwin, whom she called "ed-Win." Martha spent many hours fretting over Edwin. (Courtesy of Betty Etchison West.)

A DAY IN THE MOUNTAINS. Citizens of Mocksville traveled by train to Lenoir and then by wagon to Blowing Rock to enjoy a visit to the mountains. (Courtesy of Hugh S. Larew.)

MOUNTAIN TRIP. On a trip to the mountains, John W. Etchison and his Sunday school class pose in front of their Davie County Consolidated School bus. (Courtesy of Betty Etchison West.)

FIRST CAR IN REDLANDS. Lola Penelope Sofley stands beside the first car in the Redlands community. Her father, John Anderson Sofley, owned the car but never learned to drive. He once drove the car down the driveway from his store to his house. When he reached the house, he could not stop the car, so he ran the car into the house to stop. (Courtesy of Betty Etchison West.)

D. D. BENNETT'S GENERAL STORE. The D. D. Bennett General Store, located in the Cornatzer community, was built around 1901 by Drewry Derris Bennett and operated until 1970. The store sold hardware, dry goods, groceries, shoes, feeds, fertilizer, and general merchandise. The small boy on the left in the photograph is Herman Bennett. The third man from the left is the storeowner, D. D. Bennett. (Courtesy of James Wall.)

COUNTY HOME. In 1865, the County of Davie acquired three tracts of land that became known as the County Home tract. The first building, a wooden frame building, housed the poor. In 1905, a pest house was erected on the grounds for smallpox patients. The group of brick buildings was built in 1908. Residents who were able to work performed housekeeping chores and raised crops, hogs, chickens, and cows. In 1936, a tuberculosis cottage was built on the property. The County Home closed in 1955. (Courtesy of James Wall.)

MOCKSVILLE BOTTLING COMPANY. Beginning in 1903 and continuing for several years, the Mocksville Bottling Company, owned by Clarence Archibald, was located in the Wiley Clement Store building on Main Street. The business later located near 124 Salisbury Street. Archibald carried water, two buckets a trip, from a spring on the north side of Depot Street (1/4 mile away) to make his soda. The company produced fruit-flavored bottled drinks, including strawberry soda, and delivered them by wagon to stores in the county. The business later moved to a small building constructed by George Freezor for the bottling works. The building, known as the Pop House, stood across the street from the Davie County High School. Unfortunately, this building no longer exists. (Courtesy of James Wall.)

Visit us at
arcadiapublishing.com